Day by Day

Day by Day

A Journey into the Bible

BY James A. Hopwood

RESOURCE *Publications* • Eugene, Oregon

DAY BY DAY
A Journey into the Bible

Copyright © 2026 James A. Hopwood. All rights reserved. Except for brief quotations in critical publications or reviews, no part of this book may be reproduced in any manner without prior written permission from the publisher. Write: Permissions, Wipf and Stock Publishers, 199 W. 8th Ave., Suite 3, Eugene, OR 97401.

Resource Publications
An Imprint of Wipf and Stock Publishers
199 W. 8th Ave., Suite 3
Eugene, OR 97401

www.wipfandstock.com

PAPERBACK ISBN: 979-8-3852-6984-6
HARDCOVER ISBN: 979-8-3852-6985-3
EBOOK ISBN: 979-8-3852-6986-0

VERSION NUMBER 01/28/26

Unless otherwise noted, all quotations of Scripture are from the New Revised Standard Version Bible, copyright © 1989 by the Division of Christian Education of the National Council of Churches of Christ in the United States of America. Used by permission. All rights reserved.

Scripture quotations marked (KJV) are from The Authorized Version, or King James Version. Public domain.

Scripture quotations marked (MSG) are taken from THE MESSAGE, copyright © 1993, 2002, 2018 by Eugene H. Peterson. Used by permission of NavPress. All rights reserved. Represented by Tyndale House Publishers, Inc.

All emphases in Scripture quotations were added by the author.

The lyrics to the song "Day by Day" are from *The Hymnal of the Protestant Episcopal Church in the United States of America* (New York: Church Pension Fund, 1940). Per Church Publishing Inc., the official publisher of the Episcopal Church, the text is in the public domain.

This book is dedicated to those hardy folk in what is now Crossroads United Methodist Church in Lansing, Kansas, and Edgerton United Methodist Church in Edgerton, Kansas, for their enthusiasm, patience, and resourcefulness as we worked through earlier versions of this study in our time together.

Contents

Day by Day | 1

An Introduction to the Bible | 13

Part 1: Genesis—Where the Story Begins | 27

Part 2: Exodus—God Frees Israel from Bondage | 39

Part 3: Kingdom—The New Kingdom Rises and Falls | 53

Part 4: Disaster—Defeated Israel Is Carried into Exile | 73

Part 5: Wisdom—Sages Ponder How God Works | 95

Part 6: Gospel—God Comes Down to Earth | 115

Part 7: Witness—Jesus' Teaching Spreads Widely | 141

Part 8: Teaching—Letters Circulate the Message | 153

Part 9: Coaching—More Dispatches Carry the Word | 171

Part 10: Unveiling—Visions Show God at Work in History | 189

Day by Day

THIS BIBLE STUDY IS titled *Day by Day* in honor of an enduring song based on an even more enduring prayer. The song, of course, is "Day by Day." Its most famous incarnation is in the 1971 off-Broadway musical and 1973 movie *Godspell*. It was adapted for the musical from a hymn based on a prayer by Richard of Chichester, an ascetic British bishop who died in 1253.

Richard addressed his prayer to Jesus Christ, whom he described as his Lord, redeemer, friend, and brother. These are the lyrics we cherish, as they have appeared (with some minor variations) in more than two dozen hymnals since 1936:

> *Day by day, dear Lord,*
> *of thee three things I pray:*
> *to see thee more clearly,*
> *love thee more dearly,*
> *follow thee more nearly,*
> *day by day.*

It's a great prayer to wake up with each morning and a great prayer to guide you throughout the day. It's an especially great prayer to guide you during study of the Bible, which tells the story of God's love for us expressed most clearly and fully in Jesus Christ. These are the goals of this study: to help you to see Christ more clearly, to love Christ more dearly, and to follow Christ more nearly, day by day by day.

Day by Day offers a historical, theological, and relational survey of the big story the Bible tells. It reads every passage as contributing to the overall story, and that is the story of God's love most splendidly revealed in Jesus Christ. It is, therefore, a Christocentric, or Jesus-centered, approach to the Bible. Everything we read we filter through the lens of Jesus and the logic of the good news he bears. Not that we see "Jesus on every page," as some propose. Rather, we see everything as *pointing* to Jesus, *being fulfilled* in Jesus, and ultimately *making meaning* only in and through Jesus.

You also might describe this method of interpretation as a hermeneutic of love. It approaches its subject affectionately and charitably rather than suspiciously and antagonistically—or through a naïve "If the Bible says it, I believe it, and that settles it" form of biblicism. Approaching the Bible with a hermeneutic of love leads to the discovery that love is not only the key to proper interpretation of the Bible but the *result* of it as well.

That is what some of the greatest minds of Christian theology have always thought. The whole purpose of Scripture, Augustine of Hippo said, is to make us loving people—and if we're not more loving after reading the Bible, we're reading it wrong.[1]

The Bible is so often used as a weapon against others that I must repeat that point, even as I try to observe it myself: *If I am not more loving after reading the Bible, I'm reading it wrong.*

Everything is grounded in love, later theologians such as Thomas Aquinas agreed, because every part of creation reflects the character of the one who made it, and the reigning attribute of God is love (1 John 4:16). We see God's loving character revealed most clearly in Christ, who is the living image of God, the full reflection of God's glory, and the exact imprint of God's being (Col 1:15, Heb 1:3). "Whoever has seen me has seen the Father," Jesus said (John 14:9). Indeed, all Scripture testifies about him (John 5:39, Luke 24:25–27).

John Duns Scotus, a thirteenth-century Franciscan philosopher and theologian, spoke of the "primacy of Christ" in Scripture. Augustine is thought to have said that God speaks only one word in all the Bible, and that is the Word (with a big capital *W*) who becomes flesh in Jesus. The one Word of the Bible is Jesus.

Day by Day is intended to support you while you follow the Word and, as the apostle Paul says, your "inner nature is being renewed day by day" (2 Cor 4:16).

The Author's Perspective

As similar as this reading program is to so many others, this one is different, chiefly because of its perspective. All Bible studies are written from

---

1. Augustine, *On the Christian Doctrine* 1.36.40.

a particular perspective, a point of view. Out of ignorance or guile, some people deny that this is so. The truth is that *everything* is written from a particular perspective, and Bible studies and commentaries are no exception, *without exception*. Going in, you deserve to know *my* perspective.

This is a guide to reading the Bible that is intended to land outside the confines of pop religion. It's a plain and straightforward account of the big Bible story unencumbered by most of the ideological and theological deadweights that have become attached to it over the years, especially the last two hundred years. It will not please "conservative" Christians nor is it intended to. It also might not satisfy "progressive" Christians who have special agendas that I do not share or address here.

This study is not literalist, inerrantist, infallibilist, fundamentalist, millennialist, dispensationalist, determinist, absolutist, dogmatist, Calvinist or any other similar kind of "ist." It also is not revisionist, though many in the previously mentioned camps will claim that it is. Among other things it is *not*, it is not nationalist, communist, socialist, Marxist, fascist, capitalist, populist, anarchist, materialist, rationalist, hedonist, humanist, idealist, or individualist. If you want to call it "liberal" or "progressive," you won't hurt my feelings much, but you should be aware that I consider those terms as meaningless as "traditional" and "conservative," and I reject them as linked to phony culture-war controversies.

This study also is not especially feminist, though it is informed by feminist thought. It is not even Methodist, though I am a retired United Methodist pastor, for I don't intend to promote any Methodist doctrinal emphases here. I do hope, however, that you'll find ample evidence of a Wesleyan openness in the pursuit of spiritual truth. And though I have read various Black, Native American, Latin American, and Asian theologians, I cannot say that my thinking represents their interests especially well.

What you may or may not detect is my particular vantage point, which is that of an open-minded, white, heterosexual, university- and seminary-trained, small-town North American preacher who in a former life was a newspaper reporter and editor. For none of those things do I apologize, but I do recognize them as contributing to what I see, and what I fail to see, while reading Scripture.

You probably will notice some personal idiosyncrasies in the choice of issues that I highlight and others that I skim over lightly or ignore. Some issues simply arouse my curiosity more than others. I hope they inspire similar interest in you. If they don't, kindly shrug and move on.

About the Study

This study is intended to ignite your spirit, launch you into a frequent (if not daily) Bible reading habit, and lure you to join or form a small group of people who meet frequently to talk about what you've read.

The Bible tells many fascinating stories, but sometimes it's hard to understand what order they come in and how they all fit together.

- What does the romance of Ruth and Boaz have to do with the Jesus?
- How did ten of the twelve tribes of Israel get "lost"?
- What's the big picture?
- What's the overall "narrative arc," and where does it lead?

By the end of this study, you will have a firm grasp of who's who, as well as how each story expands our understanding of the ways God works in our lives.

The study offers fifty-two weeks of daily readings followed by notes on key passages and questions for pondering and discussion. The readings are grouped in ten thematic parts that can be combined in five volumes and shuffled for different approaches to the text.

Each day's reading normally runs from twenty-five to fifty verses and should take ten to twenty minutes to complete. Most daily readings comprise one or two continuous chapters of the Bible. On other days, the readings involve scattered bits of the story that you'll have to stitch together into a continuous narrative as you read along.

Passages marked "→ *Deeper*" take you "deeper into the story" but can be skipped if you don't have time or inclination. Occasionally the narrative refuses to fit neatly into the seven-day grid imposed on it, so I propose a "BIG DAY" of readings two or three times longer than normal. A section titled "Consider . . ." follows each list of readings. Included here are notes, commentary, and questions for thought or discussion. They cover topics of general interest, plus those of special interest to me that I think you also might find noteworthy.

As presented, the readings run straight through the Bible, from beginning to end, from Genesis to Revelation, in fifty-two segments that are convenient if you intend the study to last one year. However, you don't have to approach it "straight through," or in a year's time. In a moment, I'll offer some ideas on how to mix up those ten thematic parts in ways that you may find more helpful.

The daily reading load of this study is much less rigorous than in many other reading programs. You'll find this easier to fit into your daily schedule and easier to maintain over the long haul. Consider, too, that you can absorb only so much material at one sitting. Even the narrative parts of the Bible require closer reading and more effort than most novels. So it may be best to *limit* the amount you read each day. (That's shocking to hear, I'm sure. It seems counterintuitive. But for most of us, speed reading is inattentive reading.)

Reading slowly and carefully, you will read much of the New Testament and significant portions of the Old Testament as well. (You'll notice that readings from the New Testament are generally longer than those of the Old.) What's best is not the volume you read but the spiritual growth you will sense. You will move closer to God while cultivating a regular Bible reading habit that you can continue throughout your life in ways that move beyond this study.

Which Version?

Which version of the Bible should you use? If you have a favorite translation, one that speaks most directly to your heart, I think you should use it.

However, I strongly advise you to read a modern language version, *not* the King James Version. The antique language of the King James makes it difficult to read and even harder to understand.

I also would caution against the English Standard Version, or ESV. I know it is the darling of "evangelicals," but it is belligerently patriarchal in ways that lead me to question its overall integrity.

Dozens of other modern translations are available. Some are better than others, but most are at least adequate in how they express a sense of the original. Yes, I believe it is possible for God to speak to us even through a flawed translation!

There are basically two kinds of translation philosophies: the *formal* and the *dynamic*. The formal is popularly called "literal" because it attempts a word-for-word rendering of one language into another. But word-for-word translation is not always the most accurate because no two languages express the same concepts the same way. So some translators use a "dynamic" method to convey what the original says, rendering passages *thought for thought* rather than *word for word*.

The best translations recognize that there are times when literal translation is best and times when dynamic is best. My top translation choice describes itself as being "as literal as possible, as free as necessary." It comes in two varieties: the standard New Revised Standard Version (NRSV) or the newer NRSV Updated Edition (or NRSVue). The latter is a revised and, yes, updated version of the original. Either version is fine. Much of the time you can hardly tell them apart. Both are ecumenical works that reflect the work of scholars from diverse communities of faith.

Whatever translation you choose, you should always keep in mind that *every* translation is an interpretation. There are no "neutral" renderings of Scripture. Every reading has a particular point of view, a particular perspective. (Even God has a particular perspective. Please do not imagine or pretend that you know precisely what it is.)

Whatever translation you choose, you will get more from this reading plan if you have access to a study Bible that offers notes exploring the meaning of certain passages or ancient customs mentioned in the narrative. Some people find such notes distracting, so they prefer to read a passage the first time in a text-only edition. To get into the passage deeper, they then turn to a study Bible. If you can afford only one Bible or prefer to use only one in your daily study, stick with a text-only version.

My preferences (they don't have to become yours) are in order below:

Translation

    New Revised Standard Version (original or Updated Edition)

    Common English Bible (CEB)

    New Living Translation (NLT)

    New International Version (NIV, 2011 or later edition)

Study Bible

    SBL Study Bible (this is the HarperCollins Study Bible, updated by the Society of Biblical Literature, with NRSVue text)

    HarperCollins Study Bible (NRSV, still available)

    New Oxford Annotated Study Bible (NRSV)

    New Interpreter's Study Bible (NRSV)

CEB Study Bible

NIV Study Bible (but not before Fully Revised Edition with 2011 text)

Don't sabotage your efforts by trying to read a Bible with miniscule print or so many marginal notes and cross-references that the text itself is hard to follow. Feel free to customize your Bible for your personal use.

If you have trouble remembering in what order certain books come, don't hesitate to adorn your Bible with index tabs, or get one that comes with premade index notches. Especially when you're flipping pages back and forth looking up various passages, these devices can be helpful.

It is no sign of disrespect to mark up your Bible by underlining or highlighting passages and making marginal notes to yourself. How else are you going to remember certain things that seemed important the last time you read this passage and might seem even more important (or, shockingly, less important) now?

If you're one to make extensive notes to yourself, you may want to start a Bible reading journal. Not everyone can keep a journal of any kind. (I quit trying long ago, after several false starts.) But if journaling works for you, by all means do it.

Hints for Small Groups

Differing perspectives are not bad. In biblical interpretation, they can be quite good. You need to hear more than your own voice echoing back at you. That's why I recommend that you do this study in frequent conversation with at least one other person who is doing it at the same time—preferably two or three others. In other words, you should consider forming a study group. Begin by covenanting to do the daily readings, meet for at least an hour every week or two, participate in the discussion, and hold one another accountable to the task. It helps if you meet at the same time and place—Wednesdays at seven at Marsha's house, for example, or Tuesdays at six via Zoom.

Begin each group meeting with a prayer, asking the Holy Spirit for open minds and open hearts and for discernment of God's will in your lives. Then talk about the main themes of the week's readings; particular passages that you found significant, challenging, or puzzling; and study questions that you struggled to answer. Also consider how the readings fit in with what you have read previously.

Note: You don't have to all read the same translation. In fact, it may help if you read two or three different versions.

You may want to have a different discussion leader for each meeting, or stick with the same leader over several meetings. After a while, you will fall into a pattern that works best for your group.

Near the end of each meeting, briefly talk about how what you are learning is affecting your faith journey, then share joys and concerns in your lives. Close with a prayer that sums up your time together and asks for God's guidance with your prayer concerns.

Alternatives to "Straight Through"

Reading the Bible straight through, from cover to cover, is a fine thing, but it may not be the best thing for you. No matter how carefully Bible reading plans are designed, you may stumble when you get halfway through Exodus, and by the time you're knee-deep in Leviticus, you're *done*.

If you plug on through the morass of laws in Numbers and Deuteronomy, you are likely to hit a wall somewhere in the long, repetitive, and dismal story of Israel's kings. First and Second Samuel? OK. First and Second *Kings*? Not so much. The Chronicles doll it up a bit, but you're still reading the same sad account. And you may well ask, What does most of this have to do with Jesus?

Day by Day is designed to be lead you straight through the Bible, but it also offers other paths. The study is grouped into ten parts following certain themes or periods of history. You'll lose some sense of continuity if you mix up the order, but the variety may give you a needed break. Let's start by looking at the ten parts of the study.

Day by Day in Ten Parts

Part 1: Genesis—Where the Story Begins

Always a good place to start—four weeks.

Part 2: Exodus—God Frees Israel from Bondage

Some heavy legal stuff here but also some really good stories—five weeks.

Part 3: Kingdom—The New Kingdom Rises and Falls

More good stories and also lots of *Game of Thrones* intrigue—seven weeks.

Part 4: Disaster—Defeated Israel Is Carried into Exile

God speaks, hardly anyone one listens; a sad story—seven weeks.

Part 5: Wisdom—Sages Ponder How God Works

From Jonah to the Psalms, you will enjoy this part a lot—six weeks.

Part 6: Gospel—God Comes Down to Earth

Immerse yourself in the story of Jesus—eight weeks.

Part 7: Witness—Jesus' Teaching Spreads Widely

The story of the early church, as told in the book of Acts—three weeks.

Part 8: Teaching—Letters Circulate the Message

Paul's earliest, and some of his weightiest, letters to believers—five weeks.

Part 9: Coaching—More Dispatches Carry the Word

Other letters of the New Testament—five weeks.

Part 10: Unveiling—Visions Show God at Work in History

The book of Revelation isn't what you probably think it is—two weeks.

How to Mix It Up

One approach to thinking about this is to make five *volumes* of the ten parts.

Formation: Parts 1 and 2, Genesis and Exodus—nine weeks

Thrones: Parts 3 and 4, Kingdom and Disaster—fourteen weeks

Good News: Parts 6 and 7, Gospel and Witness—eleven weeks

Learning: Parts 8 and 9, Teaching and Coaching—ten weeks

Understanding: Parts 5 and 10, Wisdom and Unveiling—eight weeks.

Now, mix them up.

My pick: Start with *Formation* and *Good News*, move to *Learning*, then to *Understanding*, and conclude with *Thrones*, which is good history but often hard to read.

Another choice: Start with *Formation* and *Good News*, then alternate Testaments with these parts: *Teaching, Kingdom; Coaching, Disaster; Unveiling, Wisdom*.

However you do it, you can always take a weeklong break between parts. If you pause longer than one week, you may find it hard to get back into the daily reading habit. When you've done daily reading long enough, though, it may be such a helpful habit that you'll be eager to end your "vacation" from it, however long it is.

By the way, if you haven't figured it out yet, you can start this study anytime you want. An obvious starting time is January 1, but you can begin whenever works best for you. Also, "Day 1" of each week's readings can be any day of the week you choose, though starting each week on Sunday or Monday may be easiest to follow.

And, although the readings are obviously based on a weekly schedule, you can stretch things out a bit longer. Always be mindful, though, how easy it is to drift into not reading at all.

Later Journeys

Once you've gone through everything one time, you may find it valuable to do it all again—or maybe not. Try this: As you read along the first time through, circle the listing of verses that speak to you most, or record them in your Bible journal. On your second time through, concentrate on those passages that you've marked and skim or ignore the rest.

Reading the Bible

A few tips for reading:

- Read when you're alert, not sleepy or physically or mentally tired.
- Read in comfortable seating in a comfortable setting with few distractions.
- Keep a cup of coffee or tea or a glass of water handy if it helps.
- Also keep your notebook or journal and pen or pencil handy.
- Some people find it easiest to read at about the same time every day. Others prefer to make it a daily priority but leave the timing open. Do what works best for you.

- Sometimes the daily routine proves to be just too much, so you may prefer to "catch up" every three or four days in one marathon reading session. If this works for you (as it sometimes has for me), by all means do it—as long as you keep it up and don't have to push too fast through the reading.

- Always read at your normal pace. Don't try to race through it or skim. Occasionally, you may find it helpful to slow down and read a passage aloud. Remember, most Scripture was *intended* to be read aloud! Silent personal reading (even if you move your lips) is a recent innovation.

- If you are already familiar with a passage, try giving it a fresh read by using a different translation than the one you usually use.

- As you read, always look for connections—between people in each story, between people or events or ideas or themes in several stories, and, above all, between people and God. God is all about making connections.

- In each reading, look for passages that you find especially memorable, moments in the lives of the characters that you find especially telling, and decisions that strengthen or weaken relationships of characters in the story.

- Always ask, How can these readings bring me closer to God and others?

- Be wary, however, of seeking a personal application in every reading. You can learn much from the Bible because it was written *for* you (see Rom 15:4), but it was not written *to* you directly, and it's really not *about* you. You can and should become *part* of the story, but always remember that you are not the center of attention. God is.

- It's OK to wrestle with texts you don't understand or don't agree with. Maybe you'll view them differently when you return to them another day.

- It's also OK to rail at God, the way the psalmists often do, when bad things are happening in your life and Scripture offers little comfort. God can take the abuse. The main thing is to stay in relationship, to continue to "abide" with God as God abides with you, whether you feel God's presence or not (John 15:4–9).

- Begin each reading session with a prayer, asking for an open heart to respond to what God might say to you through the reading.
- Or simply say or sing,

  O dear Lord, of you three things I pray:
  to see you more clearly,
  love you more dearly,
  and follow you more nearly,
  day by day.

Feel free now to continue reading "An Introduction to the Bible" or jump directly into the daily readings, starting with part 1, "Genesis."

An Introduction to the Bible

How the Bible Came to Be

The Bible is not one book but many. That's what the word *Bible* means. It means "Book of Books." The Bible is a collection of books, an anthology, an entire library bound between two covers. The Bible that many of us know contains sixty-six books in two parts, thirty-nine in what we often call the Old Testament and twenty-seven in the New Testament.

What to call that *first* testament is a bit of a problem. For a long time, many people have objected to calling it *Old* because that implies that it's outdated and obsolete, compared with the brand-spanking-*New* part that's only two thousand years old. Alternative names are widely debated, such as First Testament, Hebrew Bible, or Hebrew Scriptures. I am almost convinced that it might be best to use Jewish Testament and Christian Testament to distinguish the two parts. Only almost. In this study, I use several titles interchangeably, though generally I call that first testament *Tanakh*, which is what it's long been called in the Jewish tradition. (More about that shortly.)

First, let's look at the concept of *testament*. A *testament* in the most common biblical sense is a covenant, an agreement between God and humans. The two parts of the Bible concern covenants that God initiated through the people of Israel and renewed for all people through Jesus Christ. A biblical testament also can be of the "last will and testament" variety, a valedictory statement or summary of faith and hope, such as Jacob's blessing of his sons in Gen 49 and Moses' blessing of Israel in Deut 33.

In its broadest sense, then, a biblical testament is a testimony to the actions of God in human life. The Bible is the authoritative and inspired record of God's revelation to us. It's a written testament to what God has done for us throughout history.

It is a rich and varied testimony. The Bible includes books of history and law and biography, poetry and songs, letters and sermons, wise sayings, and just plain stories. These books were written by many authors writing at different times, in different locations and cultures—and often from different perspectives. Their perspectives differ because God did not reveal all things to all people all at once but gradually, through specific events, and "in many and various ways" (Heb 1:1).

Whatever their differences, these authors share an abiding faith in God. We also believe that they were inspired by God so that there is a consistency in their writings beyond what even the authors knew. We believe that God can speak to us today through their writings. From the many voices of the biblical authors there emerges one clear voice, and that is the voice of God. The Bible is the written word of God (lowercase *w*) testifying to the living Word of God (uppercase *W*), who is Jesus Christ.

Tanakh

The books of the Bible's First Testament were written over a period of more than a thousand years. They were circulated individually at first, on single scrolls, and gradually were collected into groups of scrolls. At the time of Jesus, the Scriptures had three parts, described by Jesus as "the law of Moses, the prophets and the psalms" (Luke 24:44). This threefold division was retained over the centuries. Jewish Scriptures today are called *Tanakh* (tuh-NAAK). It's an acronym formed from the Hebrew words for the three main divisions—*Torah* (Teaching), *Nev'im* (Prophets), and *Kethuvim* (Writings).

The first division of Tanakh is the *Torah*, which is Hebrew for "teaching," or—less accurately—"law." These are the five books traditionally associated with Moses: Genesis, Exodus, Leviticus, Numbers, and Deuteronomy. Sometimes they're called the Pentateuch, a name that comes from a Greek word meaning "five scrolls."

The second major division is the Prophets. It is further divided into two sections, the Former Prophets and the Latter Prophets.

The Former Prophets are the books of Joshua and Judges, 1 and 2 Samuel, and 1 and 2 Kings. Christians often call these "history" books, but they are not the detached accounts we might expect from histories. They're history told from a clear point of view. They're prophetic, interpretive, history. They tell the story of the rise and fall of the kingdoms of Israel from a distinctly prophetic viewpoint that comes straight out of the book of Deuteronomy. (Basically, this viewpoint is that Israel prospers when it keeps its covenant with God and falters when it breaks the covenant.)

The Latter Prophets are the ones whose prophecies are recorded in books that bear their names—Isaiah, Jeremiah, Ezekiel, and the twelve "minor" prophets. The twelve are called "minor" not because they are less important than the others but simply because they are *shorter*. In ancient times, they were collected on one scroll called the Book of the Twelve.

The third major division, which Jesus referred to as the "psalms," is a miscellaneous collection now called the Writings. Here are books of poetry—Psalms, Lamentations, and the Song of Songs—and books of wisdom—Proverbs, Ecclesiastes, and Job. Here also are the romance novels that we know as Ruth and Esther and an apocalyptic saga called Daniel. Finally, there is more history—Ezra-Nehemiah and 1 and 2 Chronicles, possibly all by the same author.

The three parts of Tanakh reflect the order in which, over the centuries, the books were accepted as Scripture. The Torah is the most ancient collection and was the first to be accepted as authoritative. By about 200 BCE, most Jews also accepted the Prophets, which were collected on eight scrolls (four for the Former Prophets and four for the Latter Prophets). The Writings eventually included eleven scrolls, but the contents were long disputed, and various lists of its books circulated for several centuries.

Different Scriptures

The early fluidity of the "canon," or list of authoritative books, accounts for why some modern Bibles have different contents. Roman Catholic and Orthodox Bibles contain several books that are not in Protestant and Jewish Bibles. Protestant Bibles and the Tanakh follow a list of books that was endorsed by the rabbis of the Jamnia school about 90 CE. Roman Catholic and Orthodox Bibles follow a longer list derived from the Septuagint.

The Septuagint is a Greek translation of the Hebrew Scriptures that was made by Jews in Egypt starting about 250 BCE. Greek was the common language of the time, and the Septuagint was so widely used by Greek-speaking Christians that it became *the* Bible of the early church.

In Catholic and Orthodox Bibles, the extra books of the Septuagint are scattered throughout the Old Testament. If they appear in Protestant Bibles at all, they are likely grouped in a special section between the Old and

New Testaments called the *Apocrypha*. The name comes from a Greek word meaning "hidden." It was given to these books by a scholar who thought that they were too esoteric for the masses and should be read only by those who were sophisticated enough to properly interpret them.

The scholar was Jerome, who translated the Greek Septuagint into Latin about 380 CE for the Latin-speaking Roman church. Jerome's translation is known as the *Vulgate*, meaning that it was translated in the vulgar, or *common*, language. The Vulgate was the chief Bible of the Roman church for centuries.

When Protestant Reformers created their own versions of the Bible, they took Jerome's advice and reduced the disputed books to non-canonical status. For Protestants, these books are considered worthwhile reading but not inspired Scripture. In Catholic and Orthodox Bibles, these books are part of a *deuterocanon*, or second canon, of inspired Scripture.

Different Order

When the books of the Tanakh were written on individual scrolls (and later, perhaps, in *codices*, or primitive books), it didn't matter much in what order they were listed; you just found the individual book you wanted. But when the invention of modern printing allowed the many books to be compiled in a single volume, the order of the contents became more important.

Christian Bibles (Protestant, Catholic, and Orthodox alike) list the books in the order endorsed by the Septuagint. First comes Torah, then books of "history" (Judges through Chronicles), followed by books of poetry and wisdom, and finally books of prophecy.

This listing puts several of the books in better historical order, placing them more or less chronologically according to the story they tell. But it also draws an unnecessary and misleading distinction between books of "history" and books of "prophecy."

By including both "history" and "prophecy" books in the same category, Tanakh emphasizes that the writing of history and the writing of prophecy are both interpretive acts. Prophecy is primarily interpretation of events. The Former Prophets explain the history of Israel; they interpret the past. The Latter Prophets explain events as they are unfolding; they interpret the present and proclaim God's will for the future.

The New Testament

Happily, there is no real dispute today about the contents of the New Testament. It consists of four Gospels, the Acts of the Apostles, and a collection of letters, including the book of Revelation.

The canon has been more or less fixed since Archbishop Athanasius of Alexandria first listed all twenty-seven books in 367 CE. The order of the books has varied over the years, however. The Coverdale Bible of 1539 apparently was the first edition that used the order we know today. The arrangement of the letters is arbitrary—first Paul's longest and greatest letter, to the Romans, followed by other letters of Paul, the longest to the shortest, followed by the works of other writers, and concluding with Revelation.

Original Languages

Most of Tanakh was written in Hebrew, though a few parts were written in Aramaic, a variant of Hebrew that was widely spoken in the Mideast for several centuries around the time of Christ. All of the New Testament was written in Greek, although several Aramaic words are included, and some parts may have had Aramaic origins.

The Septuagint and the Vulgate were early efforts to translate the Bible into languages that were common at the time. Roman Catholic and Protestant church leaders later were reluctant to allow the Bible to be translated into the common tongue, but eventually they were pressured into allowing it. The Authorized Version, or King James Version, was one of the early English translations and soon became the most popular.

The Bible has been translated into thousands of languages, and there are many excellent versions in modern English. All of these are made from the ancient manuscripts that scholars think most reliably follow the originals. However, no copy of an "original" text is known to exist, so the reconstruction of the earliest texts continues as more reliable ancient manuscripts are discovered. Some translations are updated every few years, usually without fanfare because most changes are minor.

Modern Christian translations of Tanakh rely chiefly on the Masoretic Text, established around 900 CE, but make frequent references to the Septuagint. Obviously, the Septuagint is one language removed from the original Hebrew in the Masoretic Text. However, it also is a thousand years *older* than the Masoretic Text and therefore is useful for correcting problems that crept into the Masoretic Text during that millennial interval.

Most New Testament texts are derived chiefly from two fourth-century manuscripts, the *Codex Vaticanus*, or Vatican Codex, and the *Codex Sinaiticus*, or Sinai Codex. Comparing these with earlier manuscript fragments and later complete manuscripts, scholars have sifted through thousands of variations and assembled a text they think most closely resembles the original.

It is worth noting here that the so-called *Textus Receptus*, or Received Text, is not an ancient manuscript at all but a printed text assembled in 1516 by the Dutch scholar Desiderius Erasmus. It became the basis of the King James Version and other translations. It is not an *original* manuscript but a *reconstruction* based on several manuscripts. Erasmus had access to relatively few ancient manuscripts, and most scholars today think that his reconstruction is much less reliable than those used by modern translators. Far from being the most authoritative source of all, the Received Text is overall one of the least dependable.

How reliable are the texts we have? After all, they were hand copied for centuries, and copying mistakes are bound to happen. Thousands of variations do crop up among the many ancient manuscripts, but there are remarkably few *major* differences. Among the Dead Sea Scrolls discovered in 1947 was a copy of the book of Isaiah that was a thousand years older than any previously known copy—and the differences between them are few.

Linguistic studies continue to help us understand the texts better. But the meaning of some words remains obscure and subject to varying interpretation. So you may see the same verse translated very differently in two Bibles by two sets of translators, each trying to be faithful to the text as they understand it.

Several books were divided into two parts along the way. The books of Samuel, Kings, and Chronicles originally were each one book and fit onto one scroll each. That's because ancient Hebrew had no vowels. When the books were translated into Greek, which *does* have vowels, their length was doubled, and they had to be split in two scrolls.

Ancient manuscripts also lacked the chapter and verse divisions that we find so helpful today. These were added during the Middle Ages. Sometimes these divisions are arbitrary and land at awkward places. Still, they provide a common frame of reference—and it would not be practical to do it over and get it "right" this time.

Some printed versions of the Bible retain verse divisions so that every verse is a separate paragraph. This device can make reading choppy, and connections between verses can be lost. Most modern translations group verses into paragraphs to make reading easier and maintain sense flow, but they sometimes differ over where one paragraph ends and the next begins.

Titles, Authors, and Dates

The ancient scrolls of the Bible carried no titles. These were added along the way based on a scroll's content. Although some books state their author's name, many are anonymous, and authorship is deduced from the text or supplied by tradition. The five books of the Torah never say that they were written by Moses, but later tradition assumes his authorship and lends them his authority. Likewise, a few early commentators attributed the book of Hebrews to Paul, but many others were convinced that it was the work of someone else—just *who* they weren't sure.

Many books appear to have been edited several times by different hands, and it is not possible to determine when they reached their final form, let alone when the various strands that were woven into the final document were originally composed. Some books, such as Psalms and Proverbs, are collections of many writers, probably representing the work of several centuries.

It cannot be assumed that a book was written in the time period it describes. For example, the book of Ruth is set in the time of the Judges. However, it probably was written much later than that because it is not part of the Former Prophets but is in the later collection called the Writings. The book of Daniel also was written several centuries after the events portrayed in it, and it also is part of the Writings.

In the form that we have them, all the Gospels were written thirty or more years after the death of Jesus. However, all rely on earlier oral traditions and possibly on earlier written material. The letters of Paul are notoriously hard to date because we lack a precise chronology of Paul's life. (Luke's chronology in the book of Acts is maddeningly fuzzy at certain points.)

Many events also are difficult to date. The time of the exodus is much debated. The reigns of Saul, David, and Solomon are hard to pin down, and the dates of their successors can be calculated chiefly by figuring backward from later dates that are firmly established, such as the fall of Jerusalem. Scholars work from a bewildering web of clues (Ezekiel, happily, was careful to note the time of his visions), and they frequently discover that they need to adjust their estimations.

Happily, our faith is not based on knowing exactly when certain events transpired or who composed what book when. We trust that, however it came to us, the Bible is sufficient testimony to the work of God in our midst, and the books it preserves can lead us to greater understanding of, and closer relationship with, our Lord.

Following is a chart that compares the arrangement of Hebrew books in the Tanakh and in Protestant Bibles. You can see that neither arrangement is "perfect," and both reflect certain assumptions about the text that the other may reject. If you keep your eyes open while reading, it doesn't matter much which arrangement you prefer. But you ought to be aware of the differences and the similarities.

Arrangement of Books in Tanakh and Protestant Bible

Hebrew Canon (Tanakh)		Protestant Canon	
Torah (Teaching)	Genesis	*Law*	Genesis
	Exodus		Exodus
	Leviticus		Leviticus
	Numbers		Numbers
	Deuteronomy		Deuteronomy
Former Prophets (Prophetic History)	Joshua	*History*	Joshua
	Judges		Judges
	1 and 2 Samuel		Ruth
	1 and 2 Kings		1 and 2 Samuel
Latter Prophets (Prophetic Writings)	Isaiah		1 and 2 Kings
	Jeremiah		1 and 2 Chronicles
	Ezekiel		Ezra
	Hosea		Nehemiah
	Joel		Esther
	Amos	*Wisdom*	Job
	Obadiah		Psalms
	Jonah		Proverbs
	Micah		Ecclesiastes
	Nahum		Song of Songs
	Habakkuk	*Prophets*	Isaiah
	Zephaniah		Jeremiah
	Haggai		Lamentations
	Zechariah		Ezekiel
	Malachi		Daniel
Writings			Hosea
Wisdom	Psalms		Joel
	Job		Amos
	Proverbs		Obadiah
Festival Scrolls	Ruth		Jonah
	Esther		Micah
	Ecclesiastes		Nahum
	Song of Songs		Habakkuk
	Lamentations		Zephaniah
Other Writings	Daniel		Haggai
	Ezra-Nehemiah		Zechariah
	1 and 2 Chronicles		Malachi

Between the Testaments

The Tanakh's historical narrative stops about the time that Nehemiah led the last group of exiles home from Babylon. Many Jews never returned to their homeland but remained scattered among other nations in the *diaspora*. (The book of Esther tells a story of diaspora Jews in Persia.)

Despite their wide dispersal, many Jews remained in contact with one another. Because so few had access to the rebuilt temple, they started meeting in a *synagogue* for prayer and teaching. Eventually the synagogue became so important to Jewish religious life that it flourished even in Judea, where worship was still focused on the temple.

Many diaspora Jews could not read Hebrew, so the Scriptures were translated into Greek in the Septuagint starting about 250 BCE. The work was done in Alexandria, a new city in Egypt founded by Alexander the Great. Alexander not only conquered a large portion of the ancient world, he also made Greek the world's common language, and he set about reshaping everything in the cultural image of Greece.

This reshaping did not go well in Judea under Alexander's successors. The Seleucid dynasty's King Antiochus IV called himself Epiphanes, meaning "god made manifest." About 168 BCE, he erected a pagan altar in the Jerusalem temple and began a campaign of terror to force Jews to give up their faith and worship him. (Parts of the book of Daniel probably were written during this time to encourage Jews to keep the faith even as they had during captivity in Babylon.)

Led by Judas Maccabeus, the Jews revolted, rededicated the temple, and established an independent dynasty that lasted for nearly a century. Judea was conquered by Rome in 63 BCE. The Romans allowed the Jews great religious freedom, and the puppet King Herod the Great built the temple into one of the wonders of the ancient world, but many Jews yearned for political freedom as well, and rebellion simmered.

Open warfare began in 66 CE. It resulted in the destruction of Jerusalem in 70 CE and exile of those who survived. Now permanently deprived of the temple, Jews relied on the synagogue and study of the Scriptures. A definitive list of what books could be considered Scripture was reached by about 90 CE, not long after the formal split between Jews and Christians.

Jesus lived from about 6 BCE to 30 to 33 CE. (The old BC/AD, Before Christ / Anno Domini, time scheme is a product of the Middle Ages. It hinges on Jesus' birth but miscalculates the date.)

Jewish religious practice after the fall of Jerusalem in 70 CE was partly based on the teachings of the Pharisees, who sought to fulfill the commands of the Torah in daily life. The tone of reports in the Gospels of Jesus clashing with the Pharisees reflect the tensions both of Jesus' time and the later time when Jews and Christians were consciously separating.

Several other religious groups were important in Jesus' day. The Sadducees were aristocrats whose faith was tied to temple worship. Stability was important to them, and they openly collaborated with the Romans. The Zealots espoused armed rebellion against Rome. (One of Jesus' disciples was called Simon the Zealot, and Judas Iscariot may have been one, too.) Meanwhile, in the wilderness where John the Baptist did much of his ministry, the pietist and separatist Essenes flourished around the community of Qumran, where what we know as the Dead Sea Scrolls were produced.

It was into this rich but conflicted religious atmosphere that Jesus brought his powerful message of God's love.

Layers of Meaning

Readers have always seen multiple layers of meaning in Scripture. These go by several names but often are called the *literal*, the *allegorical*, the *moral*, and the *anagogical*. All can be appropriate ways of reading, depending on the text.

The *literal sense* is the "plain" meaning of text, what we think the author intended, as we are able to discern it. Though we call this the "plain" meaning, there is nothing "plain" about it. Many factors go into determining it:

- Genre (for example, is this poetry or narrative?)
- Literary context (within the story and the book where the story is found, as well as within the entire biblical canon; which part of which testament)
- Historical context (the date and setting of the events described, and the sometimes different date and setting of the writing itself)
- Word use and grammar
- Evidence from other literary or historical sources and archaeology

Use of the historical-critical method figures in here. By *critical* we don't mean (as is often supposed) carping, looking for errors. Rather, we mean close and careful examination using all interpretive tools available. This is classic exegesis, a faithful attempt to bring out the basic meaning of a text.

Note: There is a sharp difference between searching for the literal meaning of a passage and interpreting it literally. To read the Bible literally is to read it woodenly, depriving the text of any possibility of figurative meaning—as if Jesus might require yearly shearing because he is the Lamb of God. Everyone reads the Bible literally *some* of the time, but *no one* reads the Bible literally *all* of the time—*especially those who say that they do*.

Besides the literal meaning of a text are three "spiritual" or "fuller" layers of meaning. A text can never have *less* than its "plain" meaning, but it may mean *more*, in ways that the author may never have dreamed of. All of these three rely on figurative interpretations of a passage.

First is the *allegorical sense*. It's common for both Jewish and Christian interpreters to see the Song of Songs not as an erotic love poem but as an allegory about God's love. Referring to the story of Abraham's two sons, the apostle Paul says, "Now this is an allegory" (Gal 4:24). Paul also refers to Adam as a "type," or "pattern" of Jesus (Rom 5:14).

The early church consistently read many Tanakh texts allegorically as pointing to the coming of Jesus. In this, they followed the way Jesus interpreted the Scriptures to the two travelers on the road to Emmaus (Luke 24:27). Similarly, the Gospel of Matthew contains many typological references to show how the Old Testament anticipates the life of Jesus. These are often misunderstood as predictions ("prophecies") of what Jesus would do. What they really do is identify patterns in salvation history. They are backward references that say, "See, Jesus brings out the fuller meaning of what is prefigured in earlier Scripture."

An obvious example is when Matthew narrates how the family of baby Jesus returns from exile in Egypt to live in Nazareth. Matthew 2:15 quotes Hos 11:1: "Out of Egypt I have called my son." The prophet Hosea is clearly referring backward to the foundation of Israel, not forward to the infancy of Jesus. But Matthew sees this as a "type"—a person or event that finds its fullest expression hundreds of years later in the life of Jesus.

The *moral sense* is sometimes called the tropological sense, meaning a metaphor with a moral meaning. Paul explains this in 1 Cor 10:1–12. "Now these things occurred as examples for us" and "were written down to instruct us" (1 Cor 10:6, 11). He expands on that in Rom 15:4: "For whatever was written in former days was written for our instruction, so that by steadfastness and by the encouragement of the scriptures we might have hope." We often look for the moral sense of Scriptures, or life application, as a way of applying Scriptures today. That's a good inclination, though it can easily be misapplied and abused.

Finally, there's the *anagogical sense*. Anagogical is quite a mouthful, including two different pronunciations of the letter *g* in one word. It comes to us from the Greek word meaning "leading." Anagogical readings point or "lead" to the future, often to the promise of heaven. It's easy to use texts as a launching pad for flights of fancy rather than statements of hope that are grounded in Scripture.

These four senses of Scripture are similar to four kinds of interpretation in Judaism known as *Pardes*. These are *Peshat*, the surface or literal meaning; *Remez*, or "hint," allegorical meaning; *Derash*, meaning as parable or Midrash; and *Sod*, the spiritual or esoteric.

The rabbinic Jewish text known as the Talmud notes that a passage never loses its *Peshat*. It always keeps its plain or literal meaning. Whatever it meant to its author and original readers is basic to all other meanings derived from it.

A Bible History Timeline

Here are dates of key events, some more approximate than others:

2100 BCE	Abraham enters Canaan
1450, 1250	Possible dates for the exodus
1000	David rules the United Kingdom of Israel
970–931	Solomon succeeds David
931	The kingdom is divided
760–720	Amos and Hosea prophesy
742–701	Micah and Isaiah of Jerusalem prophesy
721	Assyrians sack Samaria, deport ten tribes
715–697	Hezekiah is king of Judah
697–642	Manasseh is king of Judah
640–609	Josiah is king of Judah; Zephaniah and Nahum prophesy

627–520	Jeremiah prophesies
597	Babylonians take thousands into exile
593–570	Ezekiel prophesies
586	Babylonians destroy Jerusalem; Obadiah, Isaiah of Babylon prophesy
539	Edict of Cyrus allows first exiles to return
520	Haggai and Zechariah prophesy
515	Rebuilding of temple is completed
445	Last group of exiles returns with Nehemiah
332	Alexander the Great controls Palestine
250	Translation of the Septuagint begins in Alexandria
168	Antiochus Epiphanes tries to wipe out Judaism
164	Judas Maccabeus rededicates temple
63	Romans occupy Palestine
37–4	Herod the Great rules under Rome
6	Jesus is born
30 or 33 CE	Jesus dies
33 or 36	Stephen is martyred, and Paul starts to follow Jesus
44	The apostle James, son of Zebedee, is martyred
48 or 49	Jerusalem Council is held
50–62	Paul writes to churches
60–62	Paul awaits trial in Rome
62	James the brother of Jesus is executed
65	Persecution begins under Nero; Peter martyred, probably Paul, too
66–70	Jewish revolt; Jerusalem destroyed
65–70	First Gospel, Mark, composed
95	John of Patmos sees heavenly visions

Enough background! Let's start reading!

PART 1

Genesis
Where the Story Begins

IN THE NEXT FOUR weeks, you will read highlights from the first book of the Bible. Genesis tells the story of human origins and the first covenants that God makes with humans. From a majestic account of creation, Genesis moves quickly into intimate tales of personal and family dysfunction as human sin spirals out of control.

Summary

    Week 1, Creation—"In the Beginning . . ."

    Week 2, Covenant—God Makes a Deal with Abraham

    Week 3, Struggle—God Transforms a Trickster

    Week 4, Dreamer—God Heals a Broken Family

The Genesis stories of creation are more concerned with the "who" than with the "how." They were written in a prescientific age and were not intended to be what we might think of as "scientific" accounts. Their primary claim is that God is creator of everything, not the gods of other nations. They present a sublime account of God bringing order to the universe simply by voice command. Other creation myths of the time involve gory battles among the gods. In these myths, humans are created to be slaves of the gods. But in Genesis humans have special status and are partners with God in the continuing creation and cultivation of the earth.

1

Creation

"In the Beginning…"

GENESIS INTRODUCES THE MAIN themes of the Bible. *Genesis* means "beginning" or "origin." The book of Genesis is about beginnings. It's about the origin of the universe, the origin of humanity, and the origin of the people of Israel. Humans are created in the image of God to mirror God's image to the world. But sin destroys the harmony of God's creation.

> Remember the Sabbath day and keep it holy.… For in six days the LORD made heaven and earth, the sea, and all that is in them, but rested the seventh day. —Exod 20:8, 11

Day 1	Gen 1:1—2:3	God creates the universe.
Day 2	Gen 2:4–25	God creates humans.
Day 3	Gen 3:1–24	Sin leads to exile.
Day 4	Gen 4:1–16	Cain kills his brother, Abel.
	Gen 4:23–24	Lamech boasts of his cruelty.
Day 5	Gen 6:5–22	God tells Noah to build an ark.
	Gen 7:11–24	God floods the land.
	Gen 8:13–19	A remnant survives.
Day 6	Gen 9:1–17	God makes a covenant with Noah.
	Gen 11:1–9	God limits human achievement.
Day 7	Ps 104	A psalm sings God's praise for creation.

Consider...

- The Gen 1 account takes a cosmic view of creation. The Gen 2 account is more intimate and relational. The accounts also differ in saying what God did when. Why do you suppose both versions were preserved for us? What does the inclusion of both versions tell you about the biblical attitude toward "contradictions" in stories?

- Who's the "us" in 1:26? Jewish tradition suggests a divine council (as in Job 1:6–12) or the "royal we." Christians see the Trinity. How do you take it?

- Genesis 1 repeatedly says that God's creation is "very good" but never calls it perfect. What would make creation better?

- What does it mean to you to be created in God's image?

- Sin is not original; God's blessing is original (1:28). Sin is a distortion of the original relationship of blessing. Do you find comfort in this distinction?

- God gives humans dominion over the earth. That makes us stewards of God's good creation. Like the first humans, our responsibility is to "till it and keep it" (2:15). In Hebrew, the words literally mean "to serve and to protect." How are we doing?

- God gives plants and animals freedom to reproduce after their own kind (1:11–12, 22, 24). They are God's subcontractors in creation. Are we also?

- All creatures are initially vegetarian (1:29–30). Later, God gives humans all animal life for food (9:3), with few of the restrictions that will later be imposed by Mosaic law. Why the looseness here and a crackdown later, do you think?

- Both male and female are created in the image and likeness of God (1:26–27). Eve is an equal partner with Adam (2:18), for partnership implies no hierarchy. How does sin later distort this relationship? Why do some people today insist on hierarchy?

- Eve often gets sole blame for disobeying God, but Adam is with her the whole time (3:6). If he disapproves, why doesn't he say or do something?

- Why is it good that Adam and Eve are kept away from the tree of life?

CREATION

- It is never clearly explained why God has "no regard" for Cain's offering. We will learn later that God accepts both plant and animal offerings, so the issue must be Cain's attitude. See the explanations of Heb 11:4 and 1 John 3:12.
- Cain is "very angry" at being rejected, and God cautions him to avoid sin. This is the Bible's first mention of the word (4:7). Aren't the earlier disobedience and blame-shifting also sinful acts?
- Cain apparently turns his anger on his brother. Why does he target Abel?
- The first death noted in the Bible is murder. Let that sink in.
- God curses the ground because of Adam's sin so that Adam must sweat to till it (3:19). Now Cain is "cursed from the ground" so that it will yield little to his tilling (4:11–12). No wonder he exclaims, "My punishment is greater than I can bear!" Despite what he has done, isn't Cain a tragic and somewhat sympathetic figure?
- The tower of Babel (11:1–9) represents the attempt to build an empire (like Babylon's) where everyone "speaks the same language" and follows the rules.
- A long life was considered a sign of God's favor. Noah lives 950 years (9:28), following the path of his grandfather, Methuselah (who lived to age 969; see 5:29), and his father, Lamech (who lived to 777; see 5:31). Note that Noah's father is *not* the Lamech of 4:23–24. We don't know how long *he* lived.
- The flood account is often presented today as a children's story. But it's very dark. Are you disturbed by the picture of God it presents?

2

Covenant
God Makes a Deal with Abraham

GOD CALLS ABRAM OUT of his homeland and tells him to journey to Canaan, a land that God will give to his descendants. Abram becomes the father of two great nations, Jews (descended from Isaac) and Arabs (descended from Ishmael).

> And he believed the LORD; and the LORD reckoned it to him as righteousness. —Gen 15:6

Day 1	Gen 12:1–9	God calls Abram.
	Gen 15:1–21	God cuts a covenant with Abram.
→ *Deeper*	Gen 13–14	Abram shows his mettle in peace and war.
→ *Deeper*	Gen 12:10–20	Abram treats Sarai shamefully.
→ *Deeper*	Gen 20:1–18	Abram again treats Sarai shamefully.
Day 2	Gen 16:1–16	Hagar gives birth to Ishmael.
	Gen 17:1–22	God seals the new covenant.
Day 3	Gen 18:1–33	Visitors promise Sarah a son.
Day 4	Gen 19:1–29	Sodom is destroyed.
Day 5	Gen 21:1–21	Isaac is born.
Day 6	Gen 22:1–19	God tests Abraham's obedience.
	Gen 23:1–4	Sarah dies.

COVENANT

Day 7	BIG DAY	*The unusual courtship of Rebekah.*
	Gen 24:1–67	Abraham seeks a wife for Isaac.

Consider...

- Abram is the first person in the Bible referred to as *Hebrew* (Gen 14:13). The word means "wanderer," "foreigner," or "outsider." It becomes an ethnic or national designation for the people of Israel. The "land of the Hebrews" (40:15) is Canaan, in which Abram and his descendants are wanderers until they occupy the land. The only portion he ever owns is a burial plot near the oaks of Mamre (Gen 23). No wonder he is so often lifted up as an example of faith!

- When he first arrives in the land, Abram builds an altar at the "oak of Moreh" near Shechem (12:6). He later builds an altar and camps more or less permanently by the "oaks of Mamre" in Hebron (13:18). The land is owned by Mamre the Amorite, a local ally (14:14). Such oak groves, or individual trees, are considered sacred for generations (35:4). Similar sites, dedicated to pagan gods, become the focus of idolatrous worship even as late as the days of Jeremiah (Jer 17:2). The path between veneration and idolatry is short, isn't it?

- The bizarre covenant ceremony of Gen 15 follows the way ancient treaties are ratified. The party with lesser power walks through a row of animal carcasses and says, "If I break this covenant, let this be done to me!" But God is the one who "walks through" the row of carcasses, not Abram. What does this mean? Who assumes the most responsibility for maintaining the covenant?

- Abraham's descendants are blessed so that they will be a blessing to others (12:1–2). As you continue this study, consider how others are blessed through Israel, and how Israel succeeds or fails to pass on the blessing it receives.

- *Deeper:* How does Abram's mistreatment of Sarai threaten his covenant with God? How is Abram *not* a blessing to Pharaoh and Abimelech? What do these episodes tell you about Abram's regard for Sarai?

- Abram and Sarai come up with their own way of making an heir, using Hagar, and they create a huge family mess. But can you blame them for losing hope?

PART 1: GENESIS

- Abram and Sarai get new names as a sign of their new relationship with God (Gen 17:5, 15). *Abram* means "exalted ancestor." *Abraham* means "ancestor of many." Both *Sarai* and *Sarah* are forms of the word "princess." Why are new names necessary or at least helpful?

- The sins of Sodom are many. (See Ezek 16:49–50 and Jude 1:7.) Why do some people focus on homosexuality? Is that the central issue, or even the issue at all, in the Genesis story? See a parallel story in Judg 19.

- Abram knows that Isaac is key to fulfillment of God's promise, yet he appears willing to sacrifice Isaac at God's command. But God's command is outrageous. Why doesn't Abraham object to it? Why does he silently go along with it? Of what must he be confident to keep such silence? What's really going on here?

- This binding of Isaac (or *Akedah* in Hebrew, meaning "binding") is often described as a test of Abraham's faith. Isn't this a rather perverse or extreme test? Doesn't God know the outcome ahead of time? If God does know, why bother with the test?

- Isaac is pretty much a cipher throughout Genesis. Granted, he is a transitional figure who lacks the charisma of Abraham and Jacob. Still, don't you wonder if his bland behavior is caused by the trauma of very nearly being sacrificed?

- Why does Abram insist on finding a wife for Isaac who's not Canaanite?

3

Struggle

God Transforms a Trickster

JACOB IS TRUE TO his name, which means "deceiver." In his first encounter with God at Bethel, Jacob agrees to worship God only if his faith is rewarded. After wrestling with God at Peniel, Jacob accepts God's blessing without reservation and receives a new name—*Israel*, which means "struggles with God," or maybe "God rules."

> Surely the LORD is in this place—and I did not know it!
> —Gen 28:16

Day 1	Gen 25:7–11	Abraham dies.
	Gen 25:19–34	Isaac and Rebekah have combative twins.
→ *Deeper*	Gen 26:1–11	Isaac follows a familiar pattern of behavior.
Day 2	Gen 27:1–40	Jacob steals Esau's blessing.
Day 3	Gen 27:41—28:5	Jacob seeks a wife.
	Gen 28:10–22	Jacob has a vision.
Day 4	Gen 29:1–30	Now Jacob is the one tricked.
Day 5	Gen 29:31—30:24	Jealous sisters grow a big family.
→ *Deeper*	Gen 30:25—31:55	Jacob feuds with Laban.
Day 6	Gen 32:3–32	Jacob wrestles with God.
	Gen 33:1–4	Jacob and Esau reconcile.

| → *Deeper* | Gen 34 | Jacob's family retaliates for Dinah's rape. |
| *Day 7* | Gen 35:9–29 | Jacob receives a blessing. |

Consider...

- Talk about a dysfunctional family! Why are Jacob and Esau such rivals?
- Why does God often favor the younger? See Paul's explanation in Rom 9:6–18. Is it God's favoritism or human favoritism that creates such havoc in these families?
- Esau is clearly dad's favorite. Why do you think Esau cares so little for his birthright?
- Jacob's name is a pun derived from "he who grasps the heel." It means "supplanter," "deceiver," "trickster." How does he live up to his name?
- After his dream at Bethel, Jacob exclaims, "Surely the LORD is in this place—and I did not know it! . . . How awesome is this place!" (28:16–17). Have you ever had a similar experience?
- Genesis 29:17 can be read to mean that Leah has "weak" eyes, or perhaps "lovely" eyes. Either way, the point is that Leah's beauty can't compare to Rachel's—at least in Jacob's eyes. How does his desire continue the story's theme of family conflict?
- Jacob and Laban are both shifty, but note how Laban resorts to increasingly dishonest tactics while Jacob seems to grow in character.
- Who is Jacob really wrestling with at the River Jabbok?
- After the encounter at the River Jabbok, God gives Jacob a new name as a sign of their new relationship. It means "one who strives with God" or "God rules." Is this a fitting name? Are you one who has strived with God, in whom God rules? Do you walk with a limp?
- Why does it take Jacob so long to come to faith in God?
- Note that the narrator makes few explicit moral judgments about the behavior of the characters in these and other stories in Genesis. Rather, the narrator leaves it to the reader to sort out the relationships of the characters and assign meaning to their actions. Does this help or hinder your understanding?

4

Dreamer

God Heals a Broken Family

As the story opens, Joseph is a favored son whose big dreams give him a big head. Soon he will be betrayed by those he loves and enslaved in a foreign land. There he will meet more betrayal and hardship. Relying on God for strength, he grows into a personal integrity that marks him for greatness.

> Even though you intended to do harm to me, God intended it for good, in order to preserve a numerous people, as he is doing today.
> —Gen 50:20

Day 1	Gen 37:1–36	Joseph's dreams get him in trouble.
→ *Deeper*	Gen 38:1–30	Tamar gets justice from Judah.
Day 2	Gen 39:1–23	Joseph is falsely accused and imprisoned.
	Gen 40:1–23	Joseph interprets dreams.
Day 3	Gen 41:1–45	Joseph rises in power.
Day 4	BIG DAY	*Joseph's brothers visit Egypt to buy grain.*
	Gen 42–43	Joseph tests his brothers' motives.
Day 5	Gen 44:1–34	Joseph continues to test his brothers.
Day 6	Gen 45:1–28	Joseph reveals his identity to his brothers.
	Gen 46:1–7	God reassures Jacob.
	Gen 46:28–33	Jacob and Joseph are reunited.
Day 7	Gen 49:29–33	Jacob dies.

	Gen 50:15–26	Joseph forgives his brothers.
→ *Deeper*	Gen 47:13–26	Joseph deals harshly with Egyptian peasants.

Consider...

- How does Jacob continue the dysfunctional behavior of his own family of origin?
- Have you ever worn what the King James Version calls a "coat of many colors" as a favored sibling—or seethed with resentment as a brother or sister wore one?
- The story of Joseph reads almost like a novel. In what will become typical "biblical style," the narrative is spare and laconic. A character's emotions are less often described than revealed through action and dialogue. In the emotional roller coaster of this story, the technique builds great reader identification with Joseph. Note how the story of Tamar and Judah heightens the tension not only by interrupting Joseph's story but also by revealing more about Judah's character.
- *Deeper:* How does Tamar use the system to her benefit in her affair with Judah? Here's a familiar story: Tamar's twins jostle in her womb (38:27–30).
- Joseph toys with his brothers, and with his father, in his dealings with them. Clearly he is conflicted in several ways. Though understandable, his behavior is hardly commendable. How could he act better?
- Joseph tells his brothers that God was behind everything (Gen 45:4–8, 50:20). Why is God mentioned so infrequently earlier in the story? What are the signs of God's activity throughout?
- Is it any wonder the Egyptians eventually turn against the Hebrews? They are shepherds who for some reason are "abhorrent to the Egyptians" (46:34). Yet Joseph convinces Pharaoh to give them "the best part of the land" (47:11).
- *Deeper:* Why does Joseph deal so harshly with Egyptian peasants?

PART 2

Exodus

God Frees Israel from Bondage

IN THE NEXT FIVE weeks, you will read how God delivers Israel from bondage in Egypt, guides the people through the desert to the promised land, and gives them a pattern of life defined by a set of laws.

Summary

Week 1, Deliverance—God Brings Israel out of Egypt

Week 2, Torah—God Teaches Israel How to Live

Week 3, Holiness—God Sets Israel Apart from Other Nations

Week 4, Wandering—A Generation Languishes in the Desert

Week 5, Formation—"Hear, O Israel . . ."

The five books of the Torah (Genesis, Exodus, Leviticus, Numbers, and Deuteronomy) are the fundamental teaching of Judaism. Through narrative and a system of rules, these books tell how to live in covenant relationship with God. At its core, this teaching is a statement of trust in God's goodness and God's providence. The readings of the next five weeks tell the formational story of Israel's foundation as a people: liberation from bondage in Egypt, a long trial in the wilderness, and reception of the Torah. Moses is the towering figure here. Guided by his unique relationship with God, Moses leads the people to new understanding of what it means to live together in freedom under God.

1

Deliverance
God Brings Israel out of Egypt

Exodus means "exit" or "departure." The book of *Exodus* tells the story of Israel's oppression in Egypt, its delivery from slavery, and its march to freedom. Exodus also tells of the laws God makes to accompany the new covenant with Israel.

> Sing to the LORD, for he has triumphed gloriously;
> horse and rider he has thrown into the sea.
> —Exod 15:21

Day 1	Exod 1:6–22	Egypt enslaves the Israelites.
	Exod 2:1–25	God hears their cries of distress.
Day 2	Exod 3:1–15	God calls Moses to lead Israel to freedom.
	Exod 4:1–17	God gives Moses signs of authority.
Day 3	Exod 4:29—6:1	Pharaoh refuses to let them go.
Day 4	BIG DAY	*And if nine plagues aren't enough . . .*
	Exod 7:1—10:29	Egypt suffers many plagues.
Day 5	Exod 12:1–39	The last plague finally convinces Pharaoh.
Day 6	Exod 14:5–31	God saves Israel at the sea.
Day 7	Exod 15:1–21	Israel praises God for deliverance.
→ *Deeper*	Ps 105, 136	Psalms praise God for deliverance.

Consider...

- Probably we all have images of the 1956 movie *The Ten Commandments* etched in our minds ("O Moses, Moses!"). As iconic as these images have become, can you see how they can distort our understanding of the story?

- How is Moses a good choice, or a poor choice, to lead Israel out of Egypt? Why does God choose him? How does God's choosing make him the right choice?

- God calls Moses out of a burning bush. Have you heard God's call to you? Was it more or less dramatic than a burning bush? How did you initially respond?

- Exodus 8:15 says Pharaoh hardens his heart against the Hebrews, but Exod 7:3 says God hardens Pharaoh's heart. Find other formulations in 10:1–2 and 14:4. Does God deliberately make Pharaoh more stubborn? Read Paul's take in Rom 9:18.

- On the night of the last plague, God "passes through" Egypt but "passes over" Israelite homes marked with lamb's blood (12:11–13). This is the origin of Passover.

- A misunderstanding or mistranslation has the Hebrews trapped at the Red Sea. It probably should be the "Sea of Reeds," a large, relatively shallow, lake near the Nile Delta. Does that make the safe crossing any less a demonstration of God's power?

- It has been argued that at least some of the plagues are similar to natural occurrences in Egypt. Yet the details of the story argue for more than natural phenomenon. For example, the narrative insists that several of the plagues are restricted to Egyptians, while Hebrews are spared.

- The number of plagues and the order in which they occur differs in the Exodus narrative compared to the accounts of Ps 78 and 105. Are the discrepancies troublesome to you? Why or why not?

2

Torah
God Teaches Israel How to Live

Torah means "teaching." Though often called "the Law" because of the many rules it contains, Torah is intended to be more a way of life than a legal code.

> The LORD bless you and keep you;
> the LORD make his face to shine upon you and be gracious to you;
> the LORD lift up his countenance upon you, and give you peace.
>
> —Num 6:24–26

Day 1	Exod 15:22–27	God leads Israel into the desert.
	Exod 16:1–3	The people grumble about hunger.
	Exod 17:1–7	The people grumble about thirst.
Day 2	Exod 19:1–9	Israel reaches the holy mountain.
	Exod 20:1–21	Ten Commandments summarize God's laws.
Day 3	Exod 32:1–35	The people grow restless and fall into sin.
Day 4	Exod 33:7–11	God speaks with Moses "face to face."
	Exod 34:1–28	God renews covenant with the people.
Day 5	Exod 22:1–31	Some laws are specific, some sweeping.
Day 6	Exod 23:1–9	These laws stress the need for justice.
	Lev 6:1–7	These laws concern restitution.

PART 2: EXODUS

	Num 15:27–31	Sins are both intentional and unintentional.
	Deut 19:15–21	Malicious witnesses face harsh punishment.
Day 7	Deut 17:14–20	Kings bear special responsibility.
	Deut 18:9–14	Magic, witchcraft, and child sacrifice are forbidden.
	Deut 18:15–22	How to judge prophets; also see Deut 13:1–5.
→ *Deeper*	Exod 25–26	Moses is told to make a portable worship space.

Consider...

- Frightened by God's voice, the people demand that Moses be their intermediary from now on (Exod 20:18–19). Have you had a similar experience?

- Why Ten Commandments? In Hebrew numerology, ten is the number of wholeness. So in ten commandments, it's all there. Anything you want to add?

- The Ten Commandments are given at Mount Horeb, which also is known as Mount Sinai because it's on the Sinai Peninsula. The first four commands deal with our relationship with God, the remaining six with our relationship with other people. Jesus' command to love God and neighbor is prefigured here. Deuteronomy 5:6–21 gives a slightly different version.

- Deuteronomy 19:21 states the "eye for an eye" principle. It was first developed in Babylon and is often known by its Latin name, *lex talionis*, the "law of retaliation." It is also mentioned in Exod 21:23–25 and explained in Lev 24:19–20 as "the injury inflicted is the injury to be suffered." Though it sounds barbaric, it is a major step forward in law because it limits the punishment that vengeful friends and relatives may demand. Still, Jesus will have none of it (Matt 5:38–42). Why is the law so memorable? Do we still interpret revenge as justice?

- God speaks to Moses "face to face, as one speaks to a friend" (Exod 33:11). The language is figurative, not literal (see Exod 33:20). Have you spoken with God so intimately?

- Exodus 22:21 and many other places require the protection of aliens in the land. If repetition is a measure of importance, this is an important command. See especially Exod 12:49, 23:9; Lev 19:33–34, 24:22; Num 15:15–16, 15:29; Deut 1:16, 10:19, 24:14, 24:17, 27:19. Why do so many Christians ignore this mandate, or work so hard against it?

- Exodus 23:4–5 commands people to do good deeds even for their enemies and those who hate them. Jesus goes so far as to command us to love our enemies (Matt 5:44; Luke 6:27, 35). Are we any closer to honoring either command?

- When we get into the mostly sordid history of Israel's kings, remember the instructions to kings given in Deut 17:14–20. Most fail miserably.

- Many provisions of the law put women at a distinct disadvantage. Numbers 5:11–28 outlines a strange ritual for when a man suspects his wife of adultery but lacks proof. Although the law gives women few property rights, Zelophehad's daughters win an important concession (Num 27:1–11 and 36:1–12). Do you think patriarchy is God's idea, or is it a human idea that's been projected onto God?

3

Holiness
God Sets Israel Apart from Other Nations

LEVITICUS MEANS "PERTAINING TO the Levites." The book of *Leviticus* is a manual for worship and a holy life. To be holy, Israel must set itself apart from other nations by its morality and its customs of ritual purity. Every aspect of life is involved, even minutia.

> I am the LORD your God; sanctify yourselves therefore, and be holy, for I am holy. —Lev 11:44

Day 1	Skim through laws of offerings for praise (Lev 1 and 2), peace (chapter 3), sin (4 and 5), and guilt (5 and 6).	
Day 2	Lev 11:1–47	Some foods are clean, others not.
Day 3	Lev 12:1–8	Ritual purity reaches everywhere.
	Lev 13:1–17	Skin diseases may also require quarantine.
	Lev 13:45–46	This "leprosy" is probably not Hansen's disease.
Day 4	Lev 16:1–34	Sins are purged on the Day of Atonement.
Day 5	Lev 18:1–30	A holy life requires purity in sexual relationships.
Day 6	Lev 19:1–37	You shall be holy as God is holy.

Day 7	Lev 25:1–55	Years of Sabbath and Jubilee are appointed.
→ *Deeper*	Lev 23	Yearly religious festivals are appointed.

Consider...

- Because it deals in legal detail, parts of Leviticus make for hard reading. If you are reading your Bible from front to back, this is where you are tempted to quit. Yet Leviticus offers many sublime passages. Name a few you encountered.

- Central to worship in Leviticus is the sacrifice of animals and grain as offerings to the Lord. These are outlined in weeks 1–5. A sacrifice is not primarily an act made to appease God (although it may have that effect) but mostly an act that acknowledges God's forgiveness.

- Leviticus contains two of the "clobber" passages used to bash homosexuals (18:22 and 20:13). Why do some people want to follow these laws but ignore others regarding clean and unclean foods, mixed fibers in clothing, length and style of beard, and tattoos?

- If God says, "You shall keep *all* my statutes" (19:37), how can we pick and choose which to follow and which to ignore? How can we *not* pick and choose?

- Clean and unclean are not moral categories. (What has God got against shellfish?) What implications does this distinction have for other commandments, such as those that we demand be obeyed while we ignore others?

- Note the male perspective throughout Lev 18. Be aware of who is dishonored by various sexual couplings and whose welfare is ignored.

- Leviticus 19 offers practical applications of the Ten Commandments. Name several.

- Given all the sacrifices going on, the tabernacle and temple must have been very bloody, smelly, messy, noisy places. Can you relate to these scenes as worship?

4

Wandering

A Generation Languishes in the Desert

THE BOOK OF *NUMBERS* gets its title from two numberings of men at the beginning and end of Israel's forty-year sojourn in the desert.

> The LORD is slow to anger and abounding in steadfast love.
> —Num 14:18

Day 1	Num 6:22–27	Israel receives a blessing.
	Num 9:1–5	Israel celebrates its first Passover in freedom.
	Num 13:1–3, 17–33	The people lose their nerve.
Day 2	Num 14:1–45	The people rebel against God.
Day 3	Num 16:1–50	Korah leads more rebellion.
Day 4	Num 20:1–13	Moses and Aaron also sin.
	Num 20:22–29	Aaron dies.
	Num 21:4–9	God provides a cure for snakebite.
Day 5	Num 21:1–3	Israel defeats the king of Arad.
	Num 21:21–26	Israel defeats the Amorite King Sihon.
	Num 21:31–35	Israel defeats the Bashan King Og.
Day 6	Num 22:1–38	A sorcerer tries to curse Israel.
	Num 23:7–12	Instead, Balaam blesses Israel.
Day 7	Num 25:1–18	Foreign gods seduce Israel.
	Num 31:1–18	Israel seeks revenge against Midian.

Consider...

- Why do the kings of Edom (Num 20:14–21), Arad, the Amorites, Bashan (21:1–35), and Moab (22–24) refuse to let Israel pass through their lands?
- At the edge of Canaan, the people falter. Is this a new timidity or the continuation of long-held insecurity? Is this why a full generation has to die before Israel can enter the promised land?
- Most of those who lived in slavery are incapable of fully understanding how to live in freedom under God. Must we also endure a long wilderness experience before we are freed from slavery to sin and we can live in freedom under Christ?
- Israel wanders in the wilderness for forty years after the forty-day mission of the spies. The number forty has great symbolic meaning in the Bible as a time of testing. Name other uses of "forty" in the story of Moses and the exodus story, and some that follow.
- How do Aaron and Moses sin at Meribah? What do they do wrong? How do you know when you are stepping out on your own authority ahead of God's authority?
- Trace the bronze snake from Num 21:9 to 2 Kgs 18:4 and John 3:14. What does this sequence of events tell you about how easy it is to fall into idolatry and miss the true meaning of God's dealings with us?
- Balaam's donkey sees better than he does. Truth or fable, isn't it a great story?
- Do you see any ethical difficulties in the story of the war against Midian?
- Men of the tribe of Levi are set aside as priests (Num 3:40–41, 44–45). They represent all firstborn males in Israel. All firstborn males are consecrated to God's service and must be redeemed from God's service by a special sacrifice (Exod 13:1–2, 11–16). Note that privilege applies only to the firstborn *male*.

5

Formation

"Hear, O Israel..."

DEUTERONOMY MEANS "SECOND LAW." It is the law restated for the new generation that will inhabit the promised land. The theology of covenant expressed here underlies the rest of the Bible. The New Testament makes nearly one hundred references to Deuteronomy.

> Hear, O Israel: The LORD is our God, the LORD alone. You shall love the LORD your God with all your heart and with all your soul and with all your might. —Deut 6:4-5

Day 1	Deut 4:1–40	"Take these things to heart."
Day 2	Deut 5:1–21	The Ten Commandments are repeated.
Day 3	Deut 6:1–25	"Hear, O Israel."
Day 4	Deut 7:1–16	"You are a people holy to God."
	Deut 9:1–7	Remember it's all God's doing.
Day 5	Deut 8:1–20	Don't forget what God did for you.
	Deut 10:12–22	A pure heart is what God wants.
Day 6	Deut 11:1–28	Here are blessings and curses.
Day 7	Deut 30:1–20	You have a choice between life and death.
	Deut 31:1–8	Joshua will succeed Moses.
	Deut 34:1–12	Moses dies.
→ *Deeper*	Deut 31:30—32:43	Moses proclaims God's steadfast love.

Consider...

- Deuteronomy has a huge influence on the rest of the Bible. When "the book of the Torah" is mentioned, Deuteronomy is most likely meant. Jesus quotes from Deuteronomy frequently.

- With its sweeping vision of God's covenant with Israel, Deuteronomy completes the Torah (the basic body of teaching central to Judaism) and sets a single standard of behavior for Israel and its kings: obedience to the covenant.

- The Shema ("Hear, O Israel"; 6:4-6) is the premiere Jewish declaration of faith. Can you see why it has been recited faithfully over the centuries?

- Torah is teaching. It is often called "the Law," and it does contain law, but it is not primarily law. It is instruction on how to walk in the way of the Lord. Torah is the way God wants us to follow because it is the way we were designed to walk, and our lives tend to be better when we walk in this path. "Happy are those whose way is blameless, who walk in the Lord's instruction," Ps 119:1 says. Psalm 119:105 adds, "Your word is a lamp to my feet and a light to my path."

- If keeping Torah means following the way of God, sin is not following the way, missing the mark, straying from the path, blundering in the dark.

- To the command to love God "with all your heart and with all your soul and with all your might" (6:5), Jesus adds "mind" (Mark 12:30, Luke 10:27). Does that cover it all?

- Moses makes it clear that every person in each generation must accept God's covenant as if God had made it with them personally (5:1-3). Do you see how important this is? Do you feel the force of such a living legacy in your life?

- In 7:1-2 (and later 20:16-18), God tells Israel to "utterly destroy" the nations occupying the land. Isn't genocide out of character for God? Evaluate this command in light of Abraham's question to God before the destruction of Sodom: "Shall not the judge of all the earth do what is just?" (Gen 18:25).

- According to 10:12–13 and 6:2, why is God's law not arbitrary? Ours is not "blind obedience" to the law but loving obedience, because we know that our loving God has our best interest in mind.
- Why is it so easy to forget what God has done for us (8:14)?
- To circumcise your heart (10:16, 30:6) is to be open to God and love God with all your heart and soul. See also Lev 26:41 and Rom 2:29.

PART 3

Kingdom
The New Kingdom Rises and Falls

THE NEXT SEVEN WEEKS are primarily history. This is not an "objective" political and economic history. It's history told from a definite point of view. This is *prophetic* history. It evaluates how well Israel follows the commands of God.

Summary

> Week 1, Conquest—Israel Invades the Promised Land
>
> Week 2, Chaos—Israel Struggles with Its Neighbors
>
> Week 3, Monarchy—Israel Gets a King
>
> Week 4, Rivalry—David's Star Rises
>
> Week 5, Royalty—David Rules as King of Israel
>
> Week 6, Division—The Kingdom Splits
>
> Week 7, Ruin—The Kingdom Disintegrates

Finally getting to the promised land, Israel struggles to settle in it and hang on to it. In the midst of chaos, the tribes turn to central leadership—a king. David is one of the Bible's greatest heroes: a mighty warrior, a sublime poet, a figure so powerful that all of Israel's future kings are judged against his standard and found wanting. His life is a mess almost from beginning to end, but he is always captivating. Those who follow his tumultuous reign never step outside his shadow.

1

Conquest
Israel Invades the Promised Land

THE BOOK OF *JOSHUA* is an idealized account of Israel's conquest of Canaan. It's named after its hero, whose name means "the Lord saves." *Jesus* is the Greek form of the Hebrew name.

> Be strong and courageous; do not be frightened or dismayed, for the LORD your God is with you wherever you go. —Josh 1:9

Day 1	Josh 1:1–11	God gives Joshua his marching orders.
	Josh 2:1–24	Joshua sends spies into the city of Jericho.
Day 2	Josh 3:1–17	The Jordan opens to allow Israel to cross.
	Josh 4:1–24	A monument is built to mark the spot.
Day 3	Josh 6:1–27	The walls of Jericho come tumbling down.
Day 4	Josh 7:1–26	Israel learns a hard lesson at Ai.
	Josh 8:1–29	Israel utterly destroys Ai.
Day 5	Josh 9:1–27	The inhabitants of Gibeon trick Israel.
Day 6	Josh 10:1–27	Israel comes to Gibeon's rescue.
Day 7	Josh 24:1–33	Israel gathers at Shechem to renew the covenant.

PART 3: KINGDOM

Consider...

- Even when the fighting is over, "very much of the land still remains to be possessed" (Josh 13:1, 18:1–3). The rest will be conquered "little by little" (Deut 7:22). It's a gradual conquest, continued even as the book of Judges opens.

- God commands that all Canaanites (and sometimes their plunder as well) are "devoted to the LORD for destruction" (Josh 6:17). This scorched-earth policy fulfills God's promise to Israel and punishes sinful Canaanites (see Gen 15:16, Exod 23:23–24, Deut 9:4–5). It also foreshadows the day when other nations will be the instrument of God's judgment on Israel. Does all the violence trouble you? Do you think God commands genocide in "holy war"? Or is Israel acting like other nations and blaming the behavior on God?

- The story of Achan's sin (7:1–26) shows how one person's actions can have great social consequences. Consider how that works in other contexts.

- When the text says the walls of Jericho come tumbling down and the sun stands still in the sky, do you take these descriptions literally or consider them to be poetic exaggeration?

- Over the next few weeks, consider the conquest of Canaan from a "liberation" perspective. Freed from slavery in Egypt, Israel gradually frees Canaan from the despotic kings who rule it. Guided by their covenant with God, Israel overthrows the rigid class system of Canaan's false gods and forms an egalitarian society based on ideals of justice and freedom for all. After a period of chaos (described in Judges), Israel establishes a new form of kingship to limit the power of rulers and preserve the rights of those who are ruled. Does this telling of the story ring true to you? (For more on this approach, see the works of Norman Gottwald and Anthony R. Ceresko.)

2

Chaos

Israel Struggles with Its Neighbors

THE BOOK OF JUDGES gets its name from heroes who "judge" Israel by holding it accountable to the commands of God and are instruments of God's deliverance in time of need. A loose alliance of tribes with local militias, Israel is easy prey for its enemies.

> In those days there was no king in Israel; all the people did what was right in their own eyes. —Judg 21:25

Day 1	Judg 2:6–23	A new generation falls into sin.
	Judg 3:12–30	Bold Ehud kills King Eglon of Moab.
Day 2	Judg 4:1–24	Deborah leads Israel to freedom.
→ *Deeper*	Judg 5:1–31	Deborah's song of victory.
Day 3	Judg 6:1–40	God calls Gideon to lead.
Day 4	Judg 7:1–25	Gideon leads three hundred men to victory.
	Judg 8:22–23	Gideon refuses an offer to be king.
Day 5	Judg 11:1–40	Jephthah achieves victory at a terrible cost.
Day 6	Judg 13:1–5, 24–25	God provides a new hero named Samson.
	Judg 16:1–30	Samson is physically strong but weak in character.

PART 3: KINGDOM

| *Day 7* | Judg 19:1–30 | In a lawless country, a woman is murdered. |
| → *Deeper* | Judg 20–21 | A terrible civil war follows this atrocity. |

Consider...

- Israel falls into a cycle of sin–redemption–faithfulness–sin that lasts for several generations. Have you had times when you can't break a destructive life pattern?

- When Joshua dies, the tribes of Israel no longer have a national leader. The stage is set for chaos. Judges twice says, "In those days there was no king in Israel. People did whatever they felt like doing" (Judg 17:6, 21:25 MSG). Why does Israel need a strong leader or "king" for leadership?

- Ehud's assassination of Eglon is one of more graphically violent stories of the Bible. The scatological details are obscured in most translations, which use language more appropriate for public reading. (When Ehud stabs him, Eglon's bowels evacuate.) This episode has been called history's first recorded locked-room mystery. Ehud's act is surely bold and dangerous, but does it strike you as "heroic"?

- Gideon is a reluctant hero. He asks for a sign involving dew and a fleece. Is needing a sign being faithless? Don't we all seek and need some kind of sign to show us that we are doing God's will?

- Why does God keep reducing the size of Gideon's army?

- Several of the judges—notably Jephthah and Samson—are greatly flawed heroes. Yet God uses even them. What does this tell you about the requirements for being chosen as one of God's champions? Does this mean God could use even *you*?

- If judges are God-appointed heroes who lead Israel back to the covenant, how does Samson fit into the picture? If there's a "hero" mold, surely he breaks it.

- What's a *shibboleth* (12:6)? Know of any today?

- Women have major roles in many stories in the book of Judges—Deborah, Jael, Jephthah's daughter, Delilah, the Levite's concubine.

Why do you suppose women play such a prominent role in this part of Israel's story?

- Scholars speak frequently of "the Deuteronomistic view of history," obviously derived from the book of Deuteronomy. In essence, it is that Israel prospers when it keeps the covenant and falters when it breaks the covenant. How do events in the book of Judges support this view—and also the view that God's love for Israel never fails?

- The story of the concubine's slaying (Judg 19) is similar to the story of the angels and Lot at Sodom in Gen 19. In both stories, lawlessness takes the form of violations of hospitality and sexuality. What does this say about social cohesion? Is sex the real issue, or is it the perverse demonstration of power over the stranger?

- What possesses Jephthah to make such a stupid vow?

- The name of the chief Canaanite god, Baal, means both "lord" and "husband." (Obviously, it's a patriarchal society.) From this "coincidence" of meaning arises the notion that when Israel breaks covenant and follows the Baals, it is whoring after other gods. This is a powerful image that will be expanded upon later, especially by the prophets Hosea (weeks 1–2) and Ezekiel (week 16) and throughout the book of Revelation in the New Testament. Can you see its strengths as a metaphor for straying from God? Can you see its weaknesses, especially as it reinforces a degrading view of women?

- Astarte (also known as Asherah or Ashtoreth) is a Canaanite goddess of war and fertility. She is often associated with Baal. An "Asherah pole" (Judg 6:25–30) might be a pole or stake, or a tree or statue.

3

Monarchy
Israel Gets a King

THE BOOKS OF *1 and 2 Samuel* tell the story of the last great judge, the priest and prophet Samuel, and the monarchy he helps establish in Israel. Like Kings and Chronicles, Samuel was originally one book. Hebrew is written with no vowels, so these books fit on one scroll. When they were later translated into Greek, which *does* have vowels, they had to be split into two scrolls—a designation that has been preserved to this day.

> But today you have rejected your God, who saves you from all your calamities and your distress; and you have said, "No! but set a king over us." —1 Sam 10:19

Day 1	1 Sam 1:1–28	Hannah prays for a child.
	1 Sam 2:1–11	Hannah dedicates Samuel to the Lord.
Day 2	1 Sam 2:18–26	Samuel grows in the Lord's favor.
	1 Sam 3:1—4:1a	God calls Samuel to service.
Day 3	1 Sam 4:1b–18	The Philistines capture the ark.
→ *Deeper*	1 Sam 5:1—7:1	The ark troubles the Philistines.
	1 Sam 7:3–14	While Samuel is judge, Israel prospers.
Day 4	1 Sam 8:1–22	Israel demands a king.
	1 Sam 9:1–20	God sends Saul to Samuel.
Day 5	1 Sam 10:17—11:15	Samuel anoints Saul as king.

MONARCHY

Day 6	1 Sam 14:1–23	Jonathan shows bravery in battle.
	1 Sam 13:3–14	Saul grows impatient and is rebuked.
Day 7	1 Sam 15:1–33	Saul disobeys and is rejected as king.

Consider...

- In the dark ages of the Judges, communication with God is rare (1 Sam 3:1). God opens a new chapter in Israel's history by providing a new hero, the last of the judges, the great prophet Samuel. God is clearly with him. The Lord "let none of his words fall to the ground" (3:19), and his authority is recognized from one end of the land to the other, "from Dan to Beersheba" (3:20).

- Samuel doesn't answer God's call at first because he doesn't realize that it is God who is calling him. Do we also sometimes fail to recognize God's call in our lives? How do we know it's God calling us and not somebody else or just our imagination? If you hear God's clear call in your life, are you willing to answer, "Here I am"?

- Raised in a dysfunctional family, Samuel creates one of his own. Both Eli's sons and Samuel's sons turn out to be scoundrels (2:12, 8:1–3). Where have we seen this pattern before? Can we ever escape the traps of family origin?

- Hannah's story is familiar—the "barren" woman who bears a child who is destined for greatness. It seems like an awful lot of trouble—why would God work this way? Find echoes of Hannah's song (2:1–10) in Mary's song (the Magnificat; Luke 1:46–55) and Zechariah's song (the Benedictus; Luke 1:67–79).

- How and why do the Israelites treat the ark of the covenant like an idol (4:2–11)?

- What great advantage in weaponry do the Philistines have (13:19–22)?

- Why do the Israelites clamor for a king (8:4–5)?

- Who are they really rejecting when they ask for a king (8:7–8)?

- The Israelites want a king "like the other nations" (8:5). But Samuel tells them that their king must be one like no other (10:25). What makes their king so different? (See Deut 17:14–20).

PART 3: KINGDOM

- Saul appears to be a good candidate for king. He's handsome, and he stands "head and shoulders above everyone else" (1 Sam 9:2). He also comes from the tiny tribe of Benjamin, so choosing him does not upset political rivalries in the larger tribes (9:21). After Samuel anoints him, God gives Saul "another heart," and he is overcome by a prophetic frenzy (10:9–13), literally seized by the Holy Spirit. (It happens again in 19:18–24.) Are you surprised by such ecstatic behavior, especially in the "Old" rather than the "New" Testament? Would you recognize such behavior if you witnessed it? Have you ever experienced it yourself?

- What events eventually cause God to reject Saul as king? (See 1 Chr 10:13–14.)

4

Rivalry
David's Star Rises

DAVID IS THE KIND of heroic figure almost everyone adores. He turns out to be everything Saul wants to be but cannot be. There is an awful inevitability about Saul's demise, and tragedy in his desperate attempt not only to save his throne but also to return to God's favor.

> Saul has killed his thousands, and David his ten thousands.
> —1 Sam 18:7

Day 1	1 Sam 16:1–23	Samuel secretly anoints David as king.
Day 2	1 Sam 17:1–51	David defeats the Philistine giant Goliath.
Day 3	1 Sam 18:1–30	Saul is jealous of David's success.
Day 4	1 Sam 19:1–17	David escapes before Saul can kill him.
Day 5	1 Sam 20:1–42	David and Jonathan are good friends.
→ *Deeper*	1 Sam 21:1–9	David seeks help from the priests of Nob.
→ *Deeper*	1 Sam 22:6–23	Saul slaughters those who helped David.
Day 6	1 Sam 24:1–22	David spares Saul's life.
→ *Deeper*	1 Sam 26:1–25	Here is a second, similar, incident.
→ *Deeper*	1 Sam 25:2–44	David spares Nabal, marries Abigail.
Day 7	1 Sam 28:3–20	Before a major battle, Saul consults a medium.
	1 Sam 31:1–13	Saul and Jonathan die in battle.
	2 Sam 1:17–27	David mourns their deaths.

PART 3: KINGDOM

Consider...

- The stories of David are among the most fondly remembered stories in the Bible. What are your favorites, and why? David and Goliath? The friendship of David and Jonathan?

- Given the winner-takes-all nature of Goliath's challenge (1 Sam 17:8–9), isn't it reckless for Saul to send young David into battle to represent Israel?

- David doesn't toss mere pebbles at Goliath but deadly missiles about the size of a baseball. Before confronting Goliath, David carefully chooses "five smooth stones" from the wadi (1 Sam 17:40). These are stones he knows he can throw with great speed and accuracy. How accurate? It was said that a good marksman could "sling a stone at a hair and not miss" (Judg 20:16).

- Who killed Goliath? David gets the credit in the familiar story in 1 Sam 17, but 2 Sam 21:19 says Elhanan did it.

- Why doesn't David kill Saul when he has the chance (1 Sam 24)? Isn't cutting off part of Saul's robe a foolhardy act?

- In the wilderness, David forms an army of outlaws and misfits (1 Sam 22:1–2). Their number soon swells from four hundred to six hundred (23:13). They hide from Saul's forces in the caves and a "stronghold in the wilderness" (23:14). The army includes "David's Mighty Men," an elite band of warriors who serve him closely. They are described in 2 Sam 23:8–39 and 1 Chr 11:10–47.

- David's exploits during his exile include pretending to be mad (1 Sam 21:10–15), raiding various enemies of Israel (23:1–29), and forming dodgy alliances with other kings, including the Philistines (27:1—28:2, 29:1–11). In other words, he's doing whatever he needs to do to survive until his insurgency succeeds.

- Rejected by God, Saul becomes increasingly unstable emotionally. The Spirit of God departs from him, and he is tormented by "an evil spirit from the Lord" (1 Sam 16:14–16). Do you find this notion disturbing? Does God torment people with evil spirits? Or is this a way of explaining otherwise unexplainable behavior?

- What do you make of the story of the "witch" of Endor (28:6–19)?

- Do you sympathize with Saul—rejected by God, tormented by an evil spirit, facing rejection by the people he leads and his own family, and judged inferior to a young hero he himself once favored?
- *Deeper:* The story of Nabal (25:2–39) parallels the story of Saul. How does the similarity reinforce David's decision to leave Saul's fate in God's hands?
- Several psalms say they were written while David was on the run from Saul. Check out Ps 34, 52, 54, 57, 59, and 142. See also Ps 63.

5

Royalty
David Rules as King of Israel

> The LORD has sought out a man after his own heart, and the LORD has appointed him to be ruler over his people.
> —1 Sam 13:14

Day 1	2 Sam 5:1–12	After a long civil war, David is anointed king of Israel.
→ *Deeper*	2 Sam 2–4	A full account of the struggle.
	2 Sam 6:1–23	The ark is brought into Jerusalem.
Day 2	2 Sam 7:1–29	God pledges to build a house for David.
Day 3	2 Sam 11:1–27	David commits grave sins.
Day 4	2 Sam 12:1–25	Nathan rebukes David.
	Ps 51	A repentant David seeks forgiveness.
Day 5	2 Sam 13:1–29	There's big trouble in David's household.
→ *Deeper*	2 Sam 14:1–33	David ignores Absalom's provocations.
Day 6	2 Sam 15:1–6, 13–23	Absalom seizes his father's throne.
	2 Sam 18:1–15	David wins the war but loses a son.
	2 Sam 18:24–33	David mourns Absalom's death.
Day 7	2 Sam 22:1–51	David sings a song of triumph (Ps 18).
→ *Deeper*	2 Sam 21:1–14	David allows vengeance against Saul's family.

Consider...

- David is an adulterer and a murderer and a lousy father to boot. How can he be considered a man "after the Lord's own heart" (see 1 Sam 13:14)?
- Michal is used and abused by both Saul and David (2 Sam 3:12–16, 6:16–23). Is it any wonder she's bitter?
- Jerusalem is an ideal capital for the tribal coalition that David is trying to cement into a single kingdom. It's centrally located but on neutral ground, associated with neither the southern nor the northern tribes. On Mount Moriah, David builds an altar (2 Sam 24:18–25) where his son Solomon will build the temple. Tradition identifies it as the place Abraham went to sacrifice Isaac.
- Is the episode with Bathsheba seduction or rape? The "good ol' boy" explanation is that Bathsheba entraps David. Can you see how ridiculous that claim is?
- David is shaken by Uzzah's death. Wouldn't you be? The rules of ark carrying are clear (Exod 25:12–14 and Num 4:15). Still, isn't God being awfully picky here?
- David wants to build a house for God, but God wants to build a royal house for David (2 Sam 7:11). Why doesn't God want David to build the temple? (See 1 Chr 22:6–10.)
- How does Nathan dare confront the king with his sins? Only in Israel, which limits the power of kings, could it happen—and even in Israel, only with a king like David.
- Any parenting lessons you can see in David's story?
- Amnon was first in line to succeed David as king, and Absalom was second, so Absalom's murder of Amnon may have involved rivalry for the throne as well as revenge for Tamar's rape. Why can't David see that before it's too late?

6

Division

The Kingdom Splits

THE BOOKS OF *1 and 2 Kings* continue the story of the monarchy through division of the empire into the Northern Kingdom of Israel and the Southern Kingdom of Judah. A parallel account in *1 and 2 Chronicles* idealizes the reigns of David and Solomon.

> I have built you an exalted house, a place for you to dwell forever.
> —1 Kgs 8:13

Day 1	1 Kgs 2:10–12	Solomon succeeds David as king.
	1 Kgs 3:1–28	Solomon pursues wisdom.
	1 Kgs 4:20–34	Solomon's kingdom prospers.
→ *Deeper*	1 Kgs 1–2	Solomon fights a bloody battle for succession.
→ *Deeper*	1 Kgs 6–7	Solomon builds the temple.
Day 2	BIG DAY	*Solomon sure sounds like he gets it.*
	1 Kgs 8:1–61	Solomon dedicates the temple.
Day 3	1 Kgs 9:1–9	God makes a conditional covenant with Solomon.
	1 Kgs 10:1–29	Solomon acquires fame and wealth.
	1 Kgs 11:1–13	Solomon falls into sin.
Day 4	1 Kgs 11:41—12:33	The kingdom is divided.
Day 5	1 Kgs 16:29—17:24	The evil Ahab becomes king of Israel.

Day 6	1 Kgs 18:1, 17–46	Elijah defeats the prophets of Baal.
	1 Kgs 19:1–18	Elijah fears for his life.
Day 7	1 Kgs 21:1–29	Jezebel steals Naboth's vineyard.

Consider...

- While 1 and 2 Samuel tell of David's rise, 1 and 2 Kings tell of the kings who follow him. Then 1 and 2 Chronicles is a rewrite of these books from the time (and perhaps the pen) of Ezra. In Chronicles, the focus is clearly on the Davidic dynasty. Other events are mentioned only as they affect David and his heirs. Some events that reflect poorly on David (such as his affair with Bathsheba) are politely ignored.

- Here's the difference between prophetic history and political and economic history. In just a few verses, 1 Kgs 16:25–27 dismisses King Omri as a failure. But secular historians of other nations call him one of the Northern Kingdom's greatest leaders and the founder of a powerful dynasty that lasts fifty years. Under Omri, the people apparently live well and prosper—but they do not honor God. As important as peace and prosperity are, they are not the best and only criterion for success, are they?

- In his rise to great wealth and wisdom and his slow descent into sin, Solomon is a legendary figure. What episodes in his life do you find most memorable?

- If Solomon is so wise, why does he mess up so badly at the end?

- After his victory over the priests of Baal, why does Elijah suddenly fear Jezebel?

- God comes to Elijah not in the wind or in the earthquake or even in the fire but "in a sound of sheer silence" (1 Kgs 19:12). Has God ever spoken to you in this way?

- What's the difference between the evils of Ahab and Jezebel? (See 21:25–26).

- Both Ahab and Jezebel will die for their evil, Elijah says (1 Kgs 21:20–24). Ahab is mortally wounded in battle (1 Kgs 22:29–38). Jezebel is killed by her own servants (2 Kgs 9:30–37). Is it satisfying or sad to see them get their "comeuppance"?

7

Ruin
The Kingdom Disintegrates

> I hate, I despise your festivals,
> and I take no delight in your solemn assemblies. . . .
> But let justice roll down like water
> and righteousness like an ever-flowing stream.
>
> —Amos 5:21, 24

Day 1	1 Kgs 22:41–44	Jehoshaphat reigns in Judah.	
	2 Chr 20:1–30	Jehoshaphat shows his faith.	
Day 2	2 Kgs 2:1–15	Elisha assumes Elijah's mantle.	
	2 Kgs 5:1–19a	Elisha leads Naaman to a cure.	
→ *Deeper*	2 Kgs 6:8–23	Elisha opens his attendant's eyes.	
Day 3	2 Kgs 8:7–15	Elisha incites revolution.	
	2 Kgs 9:1–29	Jehu sets it in motion.	
→ *Deeper*	2 Kgs 11:1–17	Israel is ruled by an evil queen.	

For a brief time under Jeroboam II, Israel is stable and prosperous, but also complacent and sinful. *Amos*, a shepherd from Judah, journeys north to proclaim God's judgment on Israel for its failure to seek social justice. At Jeroboam's death, Israel plunges into political and social chaos, and the prophet *Hosea* calls Israel to task for infidelity.

Day 4	Amos 2:6–8	Amos denounces injustice.
	Amos 4:1–3	"Cows of Bashan" are warned.
	Amos 5:4–24	Seek me and you will live, God tells Israel.
	Amos 7:10–17	Go home, Amos is told.
Day 5	Hos 1–3	Hosea sees Israel's unfaithfulness.
Day 6	Hos 4:1–3	God indicts Israel.
	Hos 5:14—6:6	Hosea calls Israel to repent.
	Hos 10:12–15	Sow righteousness, and you will reap love.
	Hos 11:1–9	God recoils at what must happen.
	Hos 13:4–11	God alone can save Israel.
Day 7	2 Kgs 17:1–34	Assyria ravages Israel and scatters its people.

Consider...

- After the kingdoms divide, it's hard to keep track of who is king in which kingdom and whether they are allies or at war with each other. The times, they are confusing.
- *Deeper*: For seven years, Judah is ruled not by a male descendant of David but by a female daughter of Israel's evil Ahab. The reign of Athaliah is noted, not fondly, in 2 Kgs 11:1–17.
- Have you ever been stubborn like Naaman? What brought you around?
- Troublemakers like Amos are often labeled as anti-government conspirators. Can you name an Amos or two from other times and places in our day? Can you name current injustices similar to those he denounces?
- Hosea writes out of his personal experience. His marriage is a parable of God's love, and the heartbreak he feels when betrayed by Gomer parallels the heartbreak God feels when betrayed by Israel. Hosea's marriage is also prophetic sign act, a symbolic way of living out prophecy. Later prophets will find their own ways of dramatizing their oracles.

- The equation of spiritual unfaithfulness with prostitution runs throughout the Hebrew Bible and into the New Testament. It is a powerful image. Does it trouble you as demeaning to women in general?
- Hosea is not afraid to mix his metaphors. After condemning Israel as a whore, he compares Israel to a lost son (11:1–9).
- Tanakh contains many references to events that happen "on the third day." The citation in Hos 6:2 was originally a metaphor describing the salvation of Israel after its punishment. It also can be interpreted as looking forward to the resurrection of Jesus.
- "What I desire is steadfast love, not sacrifice," God declares (Hos 6:6). Micah 6:6–8 offers a good parallel. What God desires is *hesed*, steadfast love, or right relationship—love similar to the undying love God has for Israel. How do we today substitute burnt offerings for steadfast love?
- Assyria's way of making sure that a conquered nation will never be a problem again is to scatter its people among other nations so that they lose their national identity as they are absorbed into the host culture. Thus the people of the Northern Kingdom become the "ten lost tribes of Israel," never again heard from in history. News of possible remnants pop up from time to time, but overall, Assyria's cruel policy succeeded.

PART 4

Disaster
Defeated Israel Is Carried into Exile

For the next seven weeks, we'll be moving between prophetic history and prophecy itself. Prophetic history evaluates events from God's perspective. Prophecy itself is not primarily prediction of the future but God's judgment (or evaluation) of behavior and where it could lead if the behavior doesn't change. The distinction blurs when the same text appears in both history and prophecy, as in Isa 38:1–8 and 2 Kgs 20:1–11; Isa 39:1–8 and 2 Kgs 20:12–19; and Isa 36:1—39:8 and 2 Kgs 18:13—20:19.

Summary

Week 1, Warnings—Judah, Too, Is Taken to Task

Week 2, Judgment—Prophets Denounce Faithless Israel

Week 3, Exile—Israel Is Carried into Captivity

Week 4, Devastation—Jerusalem Is Destroyed

Week 5, Turmoil—Israel Ponders the Unthinkable

Week 6, Comfort—Isaiah Offers Hope to the Exiles

Week 7, Return—The Exiles Come Home

As a messenger from God, the prophet's task is not chiefly to foretell the future but to proclaim God's will and declare what will happen if people don't respond faithfully. The shape of the future is not fixed by a prophecy but depends on the response to God's initiative. Jonah, for example, announces doom on Nineveh if the city does not repent—and, much to Jonah's dismay, the city repents. (For Jonah's story, see part 5.)

1

Warnings
Judah, Too, Is Taken to Task

THE SOUTHERN KINGDOM (NOW called Israel, as well as Judah) follows its own path to destruction. The prophets *Isaiah* and *Micah* issue grave warnings.

> If my people who are called by my name humble themselves, pray, and seek my face and turn from their wicked ways, then I will hear from heaven and will forgive their sin and heal their land.
>
> —2 Chr 7:14

Day 1	Isa 6:1–13	Isaiah receives a call of God.
	Isa 29:13–16	Israel's heart is far from God.
	Isa 10:1–4	Woe to those who oppress others!
	Isa 2:5–22	God's fierce day of reckoning draws near.
Day 2	Isa 1:1–31	Israel has forsaken God.
Day 3	Isa 7:1–25	Ahaz ignores a sign from God.
	Isa 8:1–10	Isaiah warns Ahaz of the consequences.
Day 4	Mic 1:1–7	Micah prophesies doom.
	Mic 2:1–4	Those who devise evil will be punished.
	Mic 3:1–4	Rulers of both kingdoms love evil.
	Mic 4:1–8	Only a remnant will see God's glory.
	Mic 6:6–8	What does the Lord require of you?

PART 4: DISASTER

Day 5	2 Kgs 18:1–37	Hezekiah looks to God for help.
Day 6	2 Kgs 19:1–37	God delivers Jerusalem from Assyria.
Day 7	Isa 20:1–6	Isaiah dramatizes Israel's folly.
	Isa 38:1–21	Hezekiah prays for recovery from illness.
	Isa 39:1–8	Hezekiah does a foolish thing.

Consider...

- The New Testament refers to Isaiah more than two hundred and fifty times.
- Can you imagine a vision as powerful as Isaiah's call?
- Micah and Isaiah of Jerusalem may be from the same prophetic school, for several of their oracles are similar (including Isa 2:2–4 and Mic 4:1–4), and both strip naked to dramatize oracles (Mic 1:8 and Isa 20:1–6).
- Micah 6:6-8 is a classic statement of prophetic faith. Why is it so memorable?
- Alternately strong and wavering, Hezekiah is one of the few kings whose personality emerges in the biblical narrative. Is he ultimately a positive or negative figure—or simply a *human* figure?
- In its original setting, Isa 7:14 says nothing of a virginal conception. The chapter opens with King Ahaz fearing an alliance of kings against him. Isaiah assures him that the alliance will collapse before a certain child is old enough to eat solid food. Ahaz panics anyway and seeks aid from Assyria, which promptly makes Judah a vassal state. The sign Isaiah offers is this: "Look, *the young woman is* with child and shall bear a son" (7:14). Seven hundred years later, the author of the Gospel of Matthew (1:23) reads this as, "Look, *the virgin shall* conceive and bear a son" (notice the shift in verb tenses). The prophecy to Ahaz concerns a normal conception. Matthew reinterprets it as a sign of the virginal conception of Jesus. In this way, Jesus' birth "fulfills" the earlier prophecy, giving it a new and deeper meaning. Do you think future events can give prophecies new meaning?

2

Judgment
Prophets Denounce Faithless Israel

THE VOICES OF *JEREMIAH*, *Zephaniah*, and *Nahum* join the prophetic chorus as King Josiah offers the last glimmer of hope for the royal line of David.

> Thus says the LORD of hosts, the God of Israel: I am going to bring such disaster upon this place that the ears of everyone who hears it will tingle. —Jer 19:3

Day 1	Isa 3:13–15	God has a case against the people.
	Isa 5:1–30	Israel is the Lord's vineyard.
Day 2	2 Kgs 21:1–16	Manasseh sets an evil course.
	2 Chr 33:10–17	Manasseh repents of his evil ways.
	2 Kgs 21:19–26	Manasseh's son Amon abandons God.
Day 3	2 Kgs 22:1–20	Amon's son Josiah wants reform.
	2 Kgs 23:1–14	Josiah destroys Judah's idols.
	2 Kgs 23:21–30	Josiah is killed in a battle against Egypt.
Day 4	Jer 1:1–19	The word of the Lord comes to Jeremiah.
	Jer 2:1–9, 21–28	Jeremiah calls on Israel to repent.
Day 5	Jer 18:1–11	God is the potter and Israel the clay.
	Jer 19:1–15	Israel will be broken like a jug.
	Jer 20:1–18	Jeremiah is persecuted.

PART 4: DISASTER

Day 6	Zeph 1:1—2:3	The day of the Lord's anger draws near.
	Zeph 3:8–20	A righteous remnant will sing God's praise.
Day 7	Nah 1:1–15	Assyria, too, will pay for its sins.
	Nah 3:1–19	Nineveh will be utterly destroyed.
→ *Deeper*	Gems from Isaiah: 4:2–6, 10:1–4, 25:9, 27:6, 30:20–21, 41:17–18, 44:21–22.	
→ *Deeper*	And from Jeremiah: 5:1; 8:7, 11, 21–22; 9:1–8; 13:24–27; 22:8–9, 15–19.	

Consider...

- The prophetic books record the sayings, or oracles, of the "writing prophets." These oracles can be bewildering because they are usually not presented in chronological order, and their context is rarely explained.

- Do you get tired of the constant badgering of the prophets? Do you see hope in them? How do you think people of their time reacted?

- Jeremiah is the longest book of the Bible, and one of the most disorienting. It's a jumble of stories and oracles, without much sense of chronological order.

- After Manasseh and Amon, Josiah is a breath of fresh air. For a brief time, it seems as if he might be able to reverse many years of apostasy and get Israel back on track with God. Sadly, it is not to be.

- Note the role of the female prophet Huldah in Josiah's story (2 Kgs 22:14–20).

- Consider the image of God as a potter and Israel as clay. What does it suggest about our relationship with God?

- See how the pottery image is reshaped. In Jer 18, Israel is compared with a clay vessel that doesn't turn out right, so the potter can rework it. God asks, "Can I not reshape you?" But in Jer 19, Israel is compared with an earthenware pot. If found defective, it can't be reshaped for a new use, only destroyed. What kind of vessel are you?

- Note how the image of the unfaithful female develops. In Jer 2:24, Israel is like a wild donkey in heat. In Nahum, Nineveh is the whore, and there is no mercy for her (3:4–7).

3

Exile

Israel Is Carried into Captivity

UNABLE TO STAND AGAINST the power of Babylon, Jerusalem falls, and thousands of people are carried into exile. Even as Jeremiah and Isaiah foresee a time when God's favor will return, both they and *Habakkuk* marvel at the harshness of God's verdict. In Babylon, *Ezekiel* warns other exiles that the worst is yet to come.

Blessed are those who trust in the LORD. —Jer 17:7

Day 1		Jer 3:6–18	God will not be angry forever.
		Jer 4:1–4	If you return to God, it will be well with you.
		Jer 17:5–10	Blessed are those who trust in the Lord.
		Jer 31:31–34	God will make a new covenant with Israel.
→ *Deeper*		Jer 26:1–24	Jeremiah is persecuted for his prophecies.
→ *Deeper*		Jer 36:1–32	King Jehoiakim burns Jeremiah's prophecy.
Day 2		2 Kgs 24:1–20	Babylon loots Jerusalem.
Day 3		Hab 1:1—2:4	Habakkuk complains, and God replies.
Day 4		Isa 64:1–12	Isaiah complains, too.
		Jer 12:1–17	Jeremiah, too.
Day 5		Ezek 1 and 2	Ezekiel hears God's call to prophesy.
Day 6		Ezek 3	Ezekiel is called to reprove Israel.

Day 7	Isa 2:1–4	Out of Zion shall go forth instruction.
	Isa 9:2–7	A righteous king shall reign.
	Isa 10:20–23	A remnant of Israel will be saved.
	Isa 11:1–12	A branch shall grow from Jesse's stump.
	Isa 32:1–8	A king will reign in righteousness.

Consider...

- God's promise of a new covenant (Jer 31:31–34) is one of the Bible's most powerful visions of God's plan for humanity. It is based on God's total transformation of the human mind and heart. Each person will know God personally and live as one who knows God's forgiveness. Wasn't this also the hope of the first covenant? Do you feel such transformation in you?

- What does it mean to circumcise your heart? (See Jer 4:4, Deut 30:6, Rom 2:28–29, and Col 2:11.)

- God tells Isaiah that a righteous king will rule Israel in "the last days" (Isa 2:2). Jeremiah says that "in those days" and "at that time," God will be enthroned in the hearts of his people (Jer 3:16, 18). Do these oracles express a hope for a long-off messianic future or a time not so distant?

- The assertion that "the righteous shall live by their faith" (Hab 2:4) is one of the most stirring affirmations of Scripture. Consider it in light of three places it is quoted in the New Testament (Rom 1:17, Gal 3:11, and Heb 10:38–39).

- To get the full flavor of the dialogue in Hab 1:1—2:4, you and another person might read it aloud in alternate sections, one reading Habakkuk's complaints and the other reading God's replies. How do God's answers sound when you hear them out loud?

- God calls Ezekiel "son of man" more than ninety times. Literally, the phrase means "son of Adam." In the sense used here, it can be taken as "mere mortal." Ezekiel is keenly aware of both the otherness of God and the sovereignty of God. The phrase will get a different turn later in Daniel and other works.

- For the hope of Jesse's tree, see Job 14:7–9.

- John of Patmos has a vision of four "living creatures" that is similar to, but not identical to, the vision reported by Ezekiel (Rev 4:6–8, Ezek 1:1–14). Ezekiel later identifies these as cherubim (10:20). The image of a "wheel within a wheel" (1:16) has fascinated artists and commentators for centuries. Apparently we are to envision one wheel slightly smaller than the other, mounted inside the other at a right angle. (It helps if you imagine the wheels as rings, without spokes.) The living creatures riding inside these wheels could thus dart in any direction without having to turn. For a stirring rendition of the vision, check out the African-American spiritual "Ezekiel Saw de Wheel" arranged by William L. Dawson.

4

Devastation
Jerusalem Is Destroyed

THE PUPPET KING ZEDEKIAH rebels against Babylon, setting the stage for the city's destruction and the exile of even more people. In Babylon, Ezekiel begins to see hope.

> The LORD, the God of their ancestors, sent persistently to them by his messengers, because he had compassion on his people and on his dwelling place; but they kept mocking the messengers of God, despising his words and scoffing at his prophets, until the wrath of the LORD against the people became so great that there was no remedy. —2 Chr 36:15

Day 1	Jer 27:1–22	Jeremiah wears a yoke.
	Jer 28:1–17	A false prophet confronts Jeremiah.
Day 2	Jer 37:1–21	Jeremiah is imprisoned.
	Jer 38:1–13	Jeremiah is thrown into a cistern.
→ *Deeper*	Jer 32:1–44	Jeremiah demonstrates his faith.
→ *Deeper*	Jer 34:8–21	Jerusalem is almost saved.
Day 3	Ezek 4 and 5	Ezekiel dramatizes what's coming.
Day 4	Ezek 8 and 9	Ezekiel sees God abandoning Israel.
	Ezek 10:1–5, 11:16–26	God's throne "moves" to Babylon.
Day 5	Ezek 24:1–24	Jerusalem is besieged.

PART 4: DISASTER

Day 6	2 Kgs 25:1–26	Jerusalem is destroyed.
	Jer 39:11–14	Jeremiah is freed from prison.
	Jer 40:1–6	Jeremiah is freed from exile.
Day 6	Jer 43:1–13	Jeremiah is hauled off to Egypt.
	Jer 44:1–30	Jeremiah denounces the idolaters.

Consider...

- Would Jeremiah be considered a traitor today, as he was in his own time?
- Jeremiah and Ezekiel both perform outrageous prophetic sign acts to get attention. Why is such odd behavior necessary? Does it help or harm their message?
- A false prophet confronts Jeremiah. How do we know he's a false prophet?
- Name some of the ways Jeremiah earns the title "weeping prophet."
- The devastation of Jerusalem is almost total. How must the people feel? What must this disaster do to their trust in God? How can they rebuild their faith?
- Even in Egypt, the refugees from Jerusalem won't listen to Jeremiah. Why won't they listen?
- Jeremiah prophesies doom, but he always holds out the hope that if people repent, God will change course and disaster won't happen after all (Jer 26:3). Prophecy is not "written in stone" but always depends on the human response to it. "Obey the voice of the LORD our God, and the LORD will change his mind about the disaster that he has pronounced against you," Jeremiah says (26:13). Whatever happens, he says, God will never abandon Israel (Jer 31:35–40).
- Refugees from Jerusalem force Jeremiah to go with them to Egypt. Scripture does not record how he dies, but tradition says that the refugees finally get tired of him and stone him to death.
- Nebuchadnezzar and Nebuchadrezzar are alternate spellings in the biblical text for the same king of Babylon, who ruled Babylon from 605 to 562 BCE. To avoid confusion, some translations always spell

DEVASTATION

the name as Nebuchadnezzar, even when the text itself has the other spelling.

- What's the significance of Ezekiel's vision of God's glory leaving Jerusalem?
- How do Ezekiel's visions show that God is "portable"? How might Israel find this notion comforting?
- Through Ezekiel, God promises, "I will give them one heart and put a new spirit within them. I will remove the heart of stone from their flesh and give them a heart of flesh so that they may follow my statutes and keep my ordinances and obey them" (11:19–20). This promise is repeated in 36:26. Compare with 18:31 and Ps 51:10. Have you felt it fulfilled in your life?
- Ezekiel's response to his wife's death is a powerful prophetic sign act (Ezek 24:15–27). God tells him not to mourn for her and to tell Israel to follow his example and not mourn the loss of Jerusalem. How do these harsh commands enable Ezekiel to speak hopefully to the exiles?
- In Ezek 8:14, the women weeping for Tammuz in the temple are performing a pagan ritual. Tammuz was a Canaanite fertility god whose consort was Asherah. His annual death and resurrection were celebrated throughout the ancient Near East. He was called Dumuzi in Sumerian mythology, where his consort was Innana, later known as Ishtar. The "queen of heaven" worshiped by Israelites in Jer 44 is Asherah, or Ishtar.

5

Turmoil

Israel Ponders the Unthinkable

A POET (TRADITIONALLY THOUGHT to be Jeremiah) moans Jerusalem's fate in *Lamentations*. The prophet *Obadiah* rails against Edom's role in Jerusalem's defeat. Ezekiel assures the exiles that God's hand of judgment will be lifted.

> How the LORD in his anger
> has humiliated daughter Zion!
>
> —Lam 2:1

Day 1	Lam 1	How lonely is the devastated city!
	Lam 2:13–22	God has humiliated Zion.
Day 2	Lam 3:19–48	God's love for Israel hasn't ended.
	Lam 5	Remember us, O Lord.
Day 3	Obadiah	Proud Edom will pay, too.
→ *Deeper*	Ezek 16:1–63	Ezekiel spins an allegory of Israel's infidelity.
Day 4	Ezek 18	The fault is your own, Ezekiel says.
→ *Deeper*	Ps 137	This psalm shows the bitterness of exile.
Day 5	Ezek 37	Ezekiel sees hope in a valley of dry bones.
Day 6	BIG DAY	*Who is this Gog?*
	Ezek 38:1–23	Ezekiel sees a new threat in Gog of Magog.

TURMOIL

	Ezek 39:1–29	Gog is defeated and Israel restored.
Day 7	Ezek 40:1–4	Ezekiel has a vision of a new temple.
	Ezek 43:1–11	Ezekiel sees God's glory returning.

Consider...

- Read Lam 1:1–9 and Ps 137 aloud. Can you understand the emotions?

- Despite its overall tone of mourning, Lamentations shows great faith in God and hope for the future, as when it proclaims, "Great is your faithfulness" (3:23). Have you had times when such faith has sustained you?

- Following conventional wisdom, the exiles complain, "Our ancestors sinned, and we bear their iniquities" (Lam 5:7). Jeremiah and Ezekiel reply, "Only the one who sins shall die" (Ezek 18:4; see also Jer 31:29–30). What's reflected in these differing attitudes?

- Consider this statement: "God forgives sin but does not remove the consequences of it." How might that be true with regard to the exiles? How might it be true in your own life?

- *Deeper:* Ezekiel 16 is a graphic allegory of Jerusalem as a prostitute who is humiliated because of her infidelity. Ezekiel 23 takes a similar turn with its tale of two wayward sisters, one representing Israel and one representing Judah. See also Lam 1:8–9.

- After the fall of Jerusalem, Ezekiel preaches hope rather than doom. His vision of the valley of dry bones (37:1–14) and victory over Gog (39:1–29) offer hope for the future. God will bring the exiles back home, reunite the two kingdoms, reestablish the line of David, and make an everlasting covenant with Israel. Though neither of these visions is time specific, can you see how they could inspire people to carry on? How did these visions prove to be true or fail to come to pass?

- Have you seen God give life to dry bones?

- Is the old animosity of Jacob and Esau revisited in Obadiah's rant against Edom?

- Ezekiel 18:5–9 offers a list of moral and ceremonial laws that are observed by a righteous person. What do you think of this summation of righteousness? Anything missing? What do you think of the rest of the chapter?

- Gog of the land of Magog (Ezek 38–39) is a mysterious figure from the north that will threaten Israel "in the latter years" (38:8) or "latter days" (38:16) but will be decisively defeated. The identification of Magog with any specific nation is purely speculative, as is any time beyond the end of an unspecified age. In Rev 20:8, "Gog and Magog" represent "nations at the four corners of the earth" that gather for a great battle at the final end of the age.

- Ezekiel 40–48 offers the prophet's detailed vision of a restored temple. Likely this vision was intended to inspire hope rather than serve as a blueprint. When the exiles return to rebuild the temple, they will not follow it as a blueprint.

6

Comfort
Isaiah Offers Hope to the Exiles

WRITING A HUNDRED AND fifty or so years after Isaiah of Jerusalem, another prophet carries on his tradition, writing in Isaiah's name to those who are captive in Babylon.

> Though I scattered them among the nations,
> yet in far countries they shall remember me,
> and they shall rear their children and return.
> —Zech 10:9

Day 1	Isa 40:1–31	Comfort, comfort my people!
Day 2	Isa 43:1–28	Do not fear, for I am with you.
	Isa 44:1–8	I will pour water on a thirsty land.
Day 3	Isa 51:1–8	God's righteousness is near.
	Isa 52:7–10	God offers comforts to Jerusalem.
	Isa 55:1–12	Come, you who thirst.
Day 4	BIG DAY	*These are the four "Suffering Servant" songs.*
	Isa 42:1–9	Here is my servant, in whom I delight.
	Isa 49:1–6	Israel will be glorified in you.
	Isa 50:4–11	If God helps me, who will find me guilty?
	Isa 52:13—53:12	My servant shall be exalted and humbled.

PART 4: DISASTER

Day 5	Isa 44:24—45:8	God has appointed Cyrus to redeem Israel.
	Isa 58:1-11	True fasting is doing justice.
Day 6	Isa 59:1-21	God will come as a redeemer to Zion.
	Isa 60:1-22	Arise, shine, for your light has come.
Day 7	Isa 61:1-11	Proclaim the year of the Lord's favor.
	Isa 65:17-25	I am about to create a new heaven and a new earth.

Consider...

- Many scholars think that the book of Isaiah is an anthology containing the work of three prophets from the same "prophetic school." These are called Isaiah of Jerusalem, who wrote most of chapters 1–39, before the exile; Isaiah of Babylon, chapters 40–55, during the exile; and Third Isaiah, chapters 56–66, after the exile. Each section has a different tone and addresses a different audience with a pertinent message for their unique situations.

- This view of Isaiah is resisted by those who see prophecy as the ability to "see" a hundred or more years into the future and deliver a message on target to that time and audience. Such a view often involves deterministic prediction—that is, events predicted far in advance that must come true because they are ordained by God to happen that way. Seeing the book of Isaiah as the work of several authors does not diminish its authority as Scripture. As with Moses and the Torah, the question is whether Scripture derives its authority from God or from a theory of authorship.

- Second Isaiah contains four songs of the "Suffering Servant" (day 4 readings). The servant is a symbol of the ideal Israel, a righteous person who represents Israel as it should be, perhaps a prophet or the coming Anointed One. Can you see parallels in the life of Jesus?

- Isaiah 61:1-4 might be a fifth servant song. Jesus quotes it (Luke 4:18-19) to refer to his mission and proclaims that the prophecy is fulfilled in him.

- Some modern accounts of Jesus' suffering mention beard pulling. Is this in the Gospel record, or is this a possibly nonhistorical inference from Isa 50:6?

- To appreciate the magnificence of several passages in Isaiah, read aloud such passages as Isa 40:12–31, 58:1–7, 61:1–7.

- For whose sake does God redeem Israel (Isa 43:25)?

- Isaiah 40:3 says, "A voice cries out: In the wilderness prepare the way of the LORD." When quoting this verse, the Gospels consistently render it, "A voice cries out in the wilderness: Prepare the way of the Lord" (Matt 3:3, Mark 1:3, Luke 3:4, John 1:23). What purpose does this change serve? How is John's call to the people of his time similar to Isaiah's call to the exiles?

- Right relation to God involves right relations with others, God says in Isa 58:1–7. Do you remember other prophets saying similar things? Is this, in fact, a central message of Scripture from the very start?

7

Return

The Exiles Come Home

THE BOOKS OF *Ezra* and *Nehemiah* tell of the exiles' attempts to resettle in their homeland. The prophets *Haggai* and *Zechariah* encourage them. Still, the reality of their situation is far from the glorious restoration envisioned by Isaiah and others.

> Thus says the LORD of hosts: "My cities shall again overflow with prosperity; the LORD will again comfort Zion and again choose Jerusalem." —Zech 1:17

Day 1	Ezra 1:1–8	Many exiles return to Judah from Babylon.
	Ezra 3:1–13	Worship resumes in Jerusalem.
	Ezra 4:1–5	Work on rebuilding the temple is halted.
Day 2	Hag 1:1—2:9	Finish work on the temple, Haggai says.
	Ezra 6:14–22	The rebuilt temple is rededicated.
Day 3	Zech 1:7–17	God is returning to Jerusalem with compassion.
	Zech 2:1–13	God again will dwell in our midst.
	Zech 3:1–10	Israel is cleansed, too.
Day 4	Ezra 9:1–15	Ezra cleans house.
	Ezra 10:1–17	The people follow Ezra's command.
Day 5	Neh 1:1—2:20	Nehemiah has a mission.

Day 6	Neh 4:1–23	Samaritans threaten the work.
	Neh 6:15–16	Nevertheless, the project is completed.
	Neh 8:1–10	Ezra reads the law to the people.
Day 7	Neh 9:1–38	Israel renews the covenant.
	Neh 10:28–39	These are among the obligations they assume.

Consider...

- They draw from many sources, but the books of 1 and 2 Chronicles, Ezra, and Nehemiah are sometimes thought to be the work of a single "Chronicler" who is often identified as Ezra. Whatever the case, Ezra and Nehemiah appear to have been combined and split apart several times, resulting in a sometimes confusing narrative.
- Even though Israel is their ancestral homeland, the exiles return to it as outsiders. The "people of the land" (Ezra 4:4) regard them as intruders; they, in turn, regard the locals as interlopers. In time, they conclude that they must remain separate from them. Why is this so important?
- Many exiles don't return at all. If your family had lived in another country for sixty years or more, how would you feel about returning to a "homeland" you never knew?
- Why would a Persian king care whether the temple is rebuilt or not?
- The rebuilt temple isn't nearly as splendid as Solomon's temple (Ezra 3:12), and people who remember the first one weep loudly over it. When Haggai insists that its glory will be greater, he may mean that people will be more faithful to God (Hag 2:9).
- Do you think Ezra's solutions to the problem of "foreign wives" is just (Ezra 10:10–11)? What about Nehemiah's attacks on them (Neh 13:23–27)?
- When Ezra reads Scripture to the people, he apparently reads in Hebrew, and others translate it into the more widely understood Aramaic (Neh 8:7–8). What does it tell you that the people have forgotten their own language?

PART 4: DISASTER

- Nehemiah must threaten to "lay hands on" violators to get them to observe Sabbath (Neh 13:15–22). Since such observance is one of the Ten Commandments, you might think it would be more widely kept.
- The Jeshua of Ezra 2:2 and Neh 7:7 is the Joshua of Hag 1:1 and Zech 3:1. *Jeshua* ("the Lord saves") is an Aramaic form of *Joshua*. The Greek form is *Jesus*.

PART 5

Wisdom

Sages Ponder How God Works

IN THE NEXT SIX weeks, we'll explore Israel's wisdom tradition, beloved stories and aphorisms, plus that great treasure of hymnody known as the psalms. If you've been doing this study chronologically, you should find this part of the study a real treat after so many weeks in grim history.

Summary

    Week 1, Inspiration—Hope for Those Who Struggle

    Week 2, Tribulation—Visions of Pain and Redemption

    Week 3, Suffering—Why Are Good People Hurt?

    Week 4, Loyalty—Three Expressions of Devotion

    Week 5, Wisdom—Aphorisms and Discerning Words

    Week 6, Worship—Israel Sings of Its Faith in God

Many of the readings for the next six weeks come from the Writings, the third of the three major divisions of the Tanakh, or Hebrew Bible. Jesus refers to this part of Scripture as "the psalms" (Luke 24:44). We'll sample the wisdom literature of the Psalms, Job, and Proverbs, and look at four of the five festival scrolls (Ruth, Esther, Ecclesiastes, Song of Songs). We'll also explore the mysterious book of Daniel, the delightful book of Jonah, and words of the prophets Joel and Malachi.

1

Inspiration
Hope for Those Who Struggle

AMONG THE MOST BELOVED stories of Scripture are those of the reluctant prophet *Jonah* and the visionary *Daniel*. The wry story of Jonah reveals the stubbornness of God's call and God's compassion for all people and creatures. The stories of Daniel's faith and courage offer an enduring example for those facing hardship and persecution.

> If our God whom we serve is able to deliver us from the furnace of blazing fire and out of your hand, O king, let him deliver us. But if not, be it known to you, O king, that we will not serve your gods and we will not worship the golden statue that you have set up.
> —Dan 3:17–18

Day 1	Jon 1–4	Jonah can't hide from God.
Day 2	Dan 1	Daniel sets boundaries for behavior.
Day 3	Dan 2:1–24	Nebuchadnezzar has a troubling dream.
Day 4	Dan 2:25–48	Daniel interprets the king's dream.
Day 5	Dan 3	Daniel's friends survive a fiery test of faith.
→ *Deeper*	Dan 4	A dream drives Nebuchadnezzar mad.
Day 6	Dan 5	Daniel interprets a sign for King Belshazzar.
Day 7	Dan 6	God saves Daniel from the lions.

PART 5: WISDOM

Consider...

- Jonah is different from other books of the prophets. It is not a collection of oracles or a biography but rather an amusing story with considerable theological punch. A prophet named Jonah was active in the Northern Kingdom just before the time of Amos (2 Kgs 14:25). However, most scholars hesitate to identify that Jonah with the Jonah of this tale, and there is no consensus on when it was written, though its apparent sympathy for Assyria suggests a later date.

- God tells Jonah to go east. Jonah goes west. Have you ever tried to run from God's call? How far did you get?

- Nineveh was the most hated city on earth. It's no wonder Jonah doesn't want to go there. Are there places *you* wouldn't want to carry God's message of salvation?

- What does the story of Jonah tell us about God's mercy?

- Did a fish or a whale swallow Jonah? Does it matter? Or is it just a big fish story?

- Jesus compares his resurrection with "the sign of Jonah" (Matt 12:39-42, Luke 11:29-32). Must we then take the story of Jonah and the fish literally? What is the real "sign" of Jonah anyway?

- The king of Nineveh says, "Who knows? God may relent and change his mind" and not destroy the city. Indeed, the narrator says that is exactly what happens (Jon 3:9-10). Consider the ramifications of the idea that God can "change his mind" and a "prophecy" may not come true because of that.

- Jonah sulks when Nineveh is spared because he thinks God has made a fool of him. "I knew you would be merciful; that's why I ran in the first place," he says (Jon 4:2). Isn't that an interesting reason for running from God?

- Daniel has two parts. Chapters 1-6 tell six court tales, mostly written in Aramaic, mostly *about* Daniel. Chapters 7-12 are apocalyptic visions, mostly written in Greek, allegedly *by* Daniel. The court tales concern a legendary figure mentioned in Ezek 14:14 and 28:3. Writing two hundred years later under Daniel's name, an unknown author uses these tales and his own visions to encourage Jews suffering under foreign rule. Though many consider it fraudulent, writing under

INSPIRATION

someone else's name is a common literary technique, then as now. The Apocrypha contains other tales of Daniel.

- The stories of Daniel refusing rich food, the fiery furnace, the lion's den, and the handwriting on the wall are among the most memorable stories of the Bible. What makes them so special? They once carried a subversive message. Do they still? What do they say about our faithfulness to God and God's faithfulness to us?

- The Babylonians give their Israelite trainees new names, just as slaveholders give new names to slaves. Why do we remember Shadrach, Meshach, and Abednego by their Babylonian names rather than their Hebrew names (Hananiah, Mishael, and Azariah)?

- Daniel's friends don't question that God *can* save them, only *whether* God will save them (3:17–18). What does this distinction tell you about faith?

- Daniel and Joseph both interpret dreams for kings. Do you see other parallels in their lives?

- Why can't Persian kings repeal an order? (See Dan 6:6–16, Esth 8:8.) Is this a sign of strength or a sign of weakness? Why can't a strong leader change his/her mind?

2

Tribulation
Visions of Pain and Redemption

DANIEL INTERPRETS EVENTS OF 168 BCE and thereafter using the highly symbolic language of apocalyptic writing. These symbols are often hard to decipher, but the theme is clear: God is in control and ultimately will triumph. The prophets Zechariah, *Joel*, and *Malachi* also look beyond hard times to days of God's triumph.

> Return to the LORD, your God,
> for he is gracious and merciful,
> slow to anger, and abounding in steadfast love,
> and relents from punishing.
>
> —Joel 2:13

Day 1	Zech 14	One day, God will reign.
Day 2	Joel 1:1–20	Rend your hearts, not your garments.
	Joel 2:1–17	The day of the Lord is coming!
Day 3	Joel 2:23–32	"I will pour out my Spirit on all flesh."
	Joel 3:1–3, 9–21	God will judge the nations and vindicate Israel.
Day 4	Dan 7:1–28	Daniel dreams of four beastly kingdoms.
Day 5	Dan 8:1–27	An angel interprets Daniel's visions.
Day 6	Dan 11:2–4	Alexander the Great's kingdom is divided.
	Dan 11:29–45	A cruel usurper (Antiochus) oppresses Israel.

	Dan 12:1–13	A great trial ends the age.
Day 7	Mal 2:10–17	Israel's unfaithfulness wearies the Lord.
	Mal 3:1–6	God is sending a messenger to prepare the way.
	Mal 4:1–5	The great and awful day of the Lord is coming!

Consider...

- These readings are examples of apocalyptic literature, a genre that is especially popular among oppressed peoples in times of persecution. In Greek, the word *apocalypse* means "unveiling." An apocalypse uses highly symbolic language to reveal hidden truths about the present to those living under oppression. Apocalyptic stories became popular among postexilic Jews when foreign domination made it clear that return to their homeland was not going to result in religious or political freedom.

- From 2:4b to 8:1, Daniel is written in Aramaic, the language most of its readers knew best. The rest is in Hebrew, which fewer readers knew well but all understood to be their native language and therefore the language of resistance to foreign oppression.

- Although it is set during the exile, part of Daniel was written much later. The Hebrew Bible places Daniel among the Writings rather than the Latter Prophets, meaning that it reached its final form long after Ezekiel and other prophets. It does not appear in a list of sacred books compiled about 200 BCE. It also reports correctly on the early reign of Antiochus Epiphanes (about 168 BCE) but incorrectly about his death (164 BCE), so that part may have been written during Seleucid oppression.

- An apocalypse doesn't necessarily have anything to do with the "end of the world," though many years of misinterpretation have cemented that meaning in pop culture. *Apocalypse* means "unveiling," not "the end." The "prophetic" parts of Daniel do not "predict" the future but interpret current events. Prophecy is interpretation, not deterministic prediction.

PART 5: WISDOM

- The four beastly kingdoms referred to in Daniel likely refer to those of Babylon (lion), Media (bear), Persia (leopard), and Greece (the ten-horned monster). Any future projection beyond these kingdoms is purely speculative, though it's likely that in the first century CE Rome was thought to be the fourth beast.

- Most of Daniel's "predictions" are so vague that anything can be read into them. Maybe that's why they're so popular with those who love to speculate about the "end times." Are you troubled by the technique or its modern application?

- "End times" talk tends to resonate most with those who have the least to lose: the oppressed, the extremely poor, those marginalized in society. Is this a longing for justice or a daydream about getting even?

- "The transgression that makes desolate" (8:13) and the "desolating sacrilege" (9:27 and 12:11) refer to Seleucid profanation of the temple with sacrifices to pagan gods. Jesus borrows this phrase when he foresees the destruction of Jerusalem (Mark 13:14, Matt 24:15).

- Are you content to know that history is in God's hands, whatever the details? If you need to know the future in detail, what room in your life is there for faith?

- Daniel lived in Babylon, a name that has become symbolic for cultures of sin and oppression. Are there modern Babylons?

- Daniel 12:2 and 12:13 are the only clear references in Tanakh to resurrection of the dead. Is this why many view Ecclesiastes and other works as pessimistic?

- In Zechariah, you can find prophecies with parallels in the life of Jesus in 9:9–10, 11:12–13, and 12:10. In Malachi, see 3:1–3, 4:1–2, 4:5–6.

- With your group or other friends, do a dramatic reading of Dan 2:26–45 and 7:2–14. Does hearing these stories aloud help you get a better feel for them?

3

Suffering
Why Are Good People Hurt?

THE BOOK OF *JOB* is one of the great works of human literature. Yet when it was written and where it is set ("the land of Uz") are uncertain.

> But I would speak to the Almighty
> and I desire to argue my case with God.
> —Job 13:3

Day 1	Job 1 and 2	God makes a deal, and Job's life falls apart.
→ *Deeper*	Job 3	Job curses the day he was born.
Day 2	Job 4:1–9	Eliphaz says innocent people don't suffer.
	Job 5:8–27	You must be guilty of something, Job.
Day 3	Job 8:1–10, 20–22	Bildad says God is always just.
	Job 11:1–20	Zophar says Job can't be innocent.
Day 4	Job 13:20–24	Help my see my sin, Job pleads.
	Job 19:7–27	"I call aloud, but there is no justice."
	Job 21:1–26	Why do the wicked prosper?
Day 5	Job 23:1–17	Job asks, "Why doesn't God answer me?"
	Job 27:1–6	Job maintains that he is righteous.
	Job 29:1–6	Job longs for the days when God loved him.

Day 6	Job 33:4–28	Elihu says God may use suffering to chasten us.
	Job 34:10–15	"God will never pervert justice."
Day 7	BIG DAY	*God speaks out of the storm.*
	Job 38–41	God answers Job's complaint.
	Job 42	Job repents, and his life is restored.

Consider...

- A literary masterpiece, Job questions conventional wisdom about God and suffering and does so in such a way that it satisfies our longing for truth without answering many of the serious questions it raises.

- The "patience of Job" is proverbial, but notice that it lasts only two chapters. Readers know that his suffering is a test of faith. Job does not know why he is suffering, and he demands some answers.

- Job's three friends sit with him in mourning for a week. When they open their mouths, they only add to Job's misery. Is there a lesson here about caring?

- Be alert when someone quotes from Job because the testimony of Job's three friends is mostly worthless conventional wisdom. Thus says the Lord, Job 42:7.

- God condemns Job's three friends but not Elihu. Does that mean that this brash young man speaks correctly?

- Job is not sinless (7:20–21), but even God admits that he is "blameless and upright" (1:1, 8). What's the difference between being sinless and blameless? How does this distinction figure into our thinking about righteousness?

- *Satan*, as used in Job 1:6, is a title, not a name. Literally, the figure is called "the Satan," or "the Accuser." He's an angel, or some other kind of exalted being, who is a member of the heavenly council. His job is to go "to and fro" on earth looking for spiritual frauds. How does this idea compare with some of our modern thinking about Satan?

SUFFERING

- "Does Job fear God for nothing?" the Accuser asks (1:9). Does he love God for who God is, or for what he can get from God? How can we be sure *our* motives are pure?

- Are you disturbed by the idea that God hands Job over to Satan on what amounts to a bet?

- Job asks, "Shall we receive the good at the hand of God and not receive the bad?" (2:10). The question assumes that God brings bad to us as well as good. What do you think? Is God responsible for everything that happens to us?

- Job is so devastated that he curses the day he was born (Job 3). Have you ever felt such despair? If you have, have you recovered from it, and how did you do it?

- "Happy is the one whom God reproves," Eliphaz says (5:17). Isn't this one of those smarmy sayings that make you want to scream? "I've just been reprimanded by God. Happy, happy, joy, joy!" So why do people keep repeating sayings like this? Why do people find comfort in them?

- Leviathan (3:8, 41:1–34) is the mythical dragon of chaos that God subdued but did not kill when bringing order to creation. Apparently Leviathan periodically breaks loose to cause problems in the world. God ultimately will slay Leviathan, says Isa 27:1. There may be some connection between Leviathan and "that ancient serpent who is called the Devil and Satan, the deceiver of the whole world" (Rev 12:9).

- "Can you fathom the secrets of God?" That's a challenge to Job from Zophar (11:7-11) and Elihu (36:29—37:24)—and, finally, from God's voice in the whirlwind (38-40). Job is silenced only by God's direct reply to him.

- What's the point of Job's story? Is it the restoration of Job's fortune, or the restoration of Job's relationship with God?

4

Loyalty
Three Expressions of Devotion

THREE BOOKS THAT EMERGED after the exile offer complementary love stories. *Ruth* and *Esther* have a common theme: loving loyalty. *Song of Songs* (also known as the Song of Solomon) is a collection of erotic poems celebrating the joys of romantic love.

> Where you go, I will go;
> where you lodge, I will lodge;
> your people shall be my people
> and your God my God.
> —Ruth 1:16

Day 1	Ruth 1	Ruth remains loyal to Naomi.
	Ruth 2	Ruth finds favor with Boaz.
Day 2	Ruth 3	Ruth asks Boaz to redeem her property.
	Ruth 4	Boaz marries Ruth.
Day 3	Esth 1–2	Esther becomes queen of Persia.
Day 4	Esth 3–5	Esther risks everything to save her people.
Day 5	Esth 6–8	Esther's boldness is rewarded.
→ *Deeper*	Esth 9:16–28	Here is the origin of the feast of Purim.
Day 6	Song 1:1–17	The lovers declare their mutual devotion.
	Song 2:1–13	He is like a gazelle or a stag.
	Song 4:1–15	There is no flaw in her beauty.

LOYALTY

Day 7	Song 5:10–16	He is all radiant and ruddy.
	Song 6:4–9	She is as lovely as Jerusalem.
	Song 7:1–9	She is graceful and beautiful.
	Song 7:10—8:2	She is full of desire for him.

Consider...

- Set in the tumultuous time of the Judges, Ruth is a romance based on a true story. Set in Persia after the exile, Esther may have some factual basis, too. Song of Songs is a timeless collection of erotic poems about two lovers. The first two are long-standing "audience favorites" among Bible readers.

- Ruth, Esther, and the Song of Songs are among the five festival scrolls (Megillah) that are read at chief religious festivals of the Jewish religious year. The other two are Ecclesiastes and Lamentations. See a common thread here?

- Ruth 1:16b–17 is often read at weddings, but sometimes only to pledge the bride's loyalty to the groom. Shouldn't both parties make the same pledge?

- By pledging loyalty to Naomi and following her to Israel, Ruth changes her fundamental identity, from Moabite to Israelite, from one family to another, from one set of gods to one God. Can you even imagine such a change in your life?

- Does Ruth seduce Boaz on the threshing floor? The full significance of her "uncovering his feet" is not clear, but it's hard not to see sexual overtones in it.

- A kinsman redeemer is a male whose responsibility includes buying back (redeeming) the property of family members that was sold in time of hardship. He also must marry a brother's widow to provide an heir (see Lev 25:25, 47–49; Deut 25:5–10; and the story of Tamar in Gen 38). God is viewed as Israel's kinsman redeemer (Isa 43:1, for example.) In the New Testament, Jesus is kinsman redeemer to all the world.

- Moabites, descendants of Lot, were forbidden from the assembly of the Lord "even to the tenth generation" (Deut 23:3). Yet when Moab-born Ruth bears a child, the women of Bethlehem consider him the offspring of Naomi (Ruth 4:14–17), part of their community. Are they ignoring the law or seeing beyond it?

- How is Queen Vashti way ahead of her time? She has become a feminist icon, but she was widely reviled by early male commentators of the text, and she sometimes gets the same treatment today from "conservative" readers.
- Ahasuerus commands all women in the kingdom to be subservient to their husbands (Esth 1:22). Coming from an egotistical absolute monarch, isn't this a rather weak response to Vashti's slight?
- Esther becomes queen by winning a beauty pageant. She is part of a harem. Isn't this an unsavory role for a biblical figure?
- Jews slaughter those who would persecute them. Does their apparent delight in the act make you uncomfortable?
- Esther's comment, "If I perish, I perish" (Esth 4:16), is similar to the attitude of Shadrach, Meshach, and Abednego when they face the fiery furnace (Dan 3:17). What does this tell you about the nature of faith?
- Song of Songs is often interpreted allegorically so that the meaning is more spiritual than sexual. If sex is part of God's good creation, why shouldn't there be an erotic poem in the Bible?
- The metaphors for beauty in Song of Songs come from a different culture than ours, one that's obviously rural: eyes like doves (4:1, 5:12); teeth like a flock of shorn ewes (4:2); hair like a flock of goats (6:5); breasts like two fawns (4:5, 7:3).

5

Wisdom

Aphorisms and Discerning Words

THE BOOK OF *PROVERBS* is a collection of more than a thousand traditional sayings and adages, many based on human experience rather than on revelation from God. Parts of the book are attributed to Solomon, who may have begun the collection process. He's also been credited for *Ecclesiastes*, though most scholars doubt that he had a hand in it.

> The LORD by wisdom founded the earth;
> by understanding he established the heavens;
> by his knowledge the deeps broke open,
> and the clouds drop down the dew.
> —Prov 3:19–20

Day 1	Prov 1:1–19	Reverence for God is the basis of wisdom.
	Prov 3:1–20	Wisdom is personified as a woman.
Day 2	Prov 1:20–33	Lady Wisdom makes a case for truth.
	Prov 8:1–36	"I was there at the very beginning."
Day 3	Prov 6–26	*Read at random to get the flavor of it, or follow some suggestions given later.*
Day 4	Prov 31:10–31	The perfect wife is quite a woman.
Day 5	Eccl 1	Life is meaningless vanity.
	Eccl 2:1–16	Wisdom, pleasure, folly—all are vanity.
Day 6	Eccl 2:17–26	Your toil is fruitless.
	Eccl 3	To everything there is a season.

PART 5: WISDOM

Day 7	Eccl 5:8–20	Wealth will get you nowhere.
	Eccl 9:1–12	Death is a fate common to all.
	Eccl 11:8—12:13	Praise God and be happy.

Consider...

- The Proverbs offer practical advice for daily living, distilled from life experience, from observation and reflection on life, and from revelation by God (Prov 2:6). They are intended to transmit important life skills from one generation to the next (1:8). They can be both inspiring and cloying. Your overall response to them?

- Wisdom starts with "the fear of the Lord," Prov 1:7 says. Are we supposed to be afraid of God, or reverently awed by God? Or maybe a bit of both? Are you afraid of your earthly father? Why should you be afraid of your Heavenly Father?

- Solomon was famed for his wisdom, but only some of the wise sayings in Proverbs are specifically said to be from him. These are 10:1—22:16 and chapters 25–29.

- The "thirty wise sayings" of 22:17—24:22 come from the "Instruction of Amenemope," an Egyptian book of wisdom written long before Solomon's time. Are you bothered by the notion that a book of the Bible includes Egyptian wisdom literature? Why or why not?

- Here's a sampling of familiar proverbs and some not too familiar: 6:16–19; 11:1, 7, 10; 12:19, 22, 25; 13:11, 20, 24; 14:12, 20; 15:1, 3, 9, 15, 16; 16:2, 18; 17:3, 5, 8, 12, 28; 18:10; 19:17, 21; 20:9; 21:2, 3, 13; 22:2, 6, 22–23; 24:29; 25:6–7, 21–22; 26:27; 27:1, 17; 29:2; 30:7–9.

- Proverbs 26:4 and 26:5 contradict each other. What does that mean? Does such discernment require wisdom?

- Lady Wisdom, or Sophia (Prov 8:2–31), is an embodiment and personification of wisdom. Jewish philosophers later identified Wisdom with the Greek concept of *logos* or "word," the order behind creation. The Gospel of John (1:1–3) identifies Christ as "the Word" who created all things. Can the created female Wisdom and the uncreated male Word coexist peacefully in your universe?

- Know someone who fits the job description for the "capable" wife of Prov 31?
- *Ecclesiastes* is a Greek form of the Hebrew *Qohelet*, meaning "leader of an assembly." It is commonly rendered as Teacher or Preacher or even Seeker.
- The author identifies himself as son of King David and ruler over Israel in Jerusalem. Historically, only Solomon can make these claims. Yet most scholars say the late style of its Hebrew testify that this book reached its final form much later.
- Against the sturdy and optimistic pragmatism of the Proverbs, Ecclesiastes offers unconventional candor that some readers don't welcome. Your response to it?
- Ecclesiastes can be a real downer, yet 3:1–8 ("a time for everything") is inspiring. How can such sublime thought emerge from such skepticism?
- The basic complaint of Ecclesiastes is that life isn't fair. What's your take?
- Ecclesiastes advises moderation in all things (7:15–18). Good advice?
- Ecclesiastes 9:7 basically says "Eat, drink, and be merry." Are you surprised to find such advice in the Bible? Is this libertine, or a cheerful acceptance of life's vagaries?
- The whims of time and chance can undo the best of us, Eccl 9:11 says. Is this true in your experience?
- Ecclesiastes entertains no hope of an afterlife. All who die find a shade existence in *sheol*. Therefore, the author concludes (9:4), it is better to be a live dog (gentile) than a dead lion (Jew). Do you think his attitude would be different if he believed in an afterlife?

6

Worship

Israel Sings of Its Faith in God

THE *PSALMS* ARE TORAH in song, holy instruction set to verse and music. The five books (1–41, 42–72, 73–89, 90–106, 107–150) reflect the five-fold Torah as well as the order in which the psalms were collected. The New Testament quotes the Psalms more than any other book of Scripture. In his *Preface to the Psalter*, Martin Luther calls them "a little Bible" because they encapsulate the whole.[1] Many are by David but by no means all.

> Happy are those whose way is blameless,
> who walk in the law of the LORD.
> —Ps 119:1

Read some or all of psalms listed, as you have time and inclination.

Day 1	Pss 1, 25, 32, 34, 47, 60, 90	Psalms of Torah, or instruction.
Day 2	Pss 8, 19, 29, 84, 110, 144	Psalms proclaiming God's majesty.
Day 3	Pss 2, 47, 89, 93, 95–99	Psalms extolling the reign of God.
Day 4	Pss 3, 13, 22, 38, 51, 137	Psalms of lament or supplication.
Day 5	Pss 84, 100, 145, 146	Psalms of praise.

---

1. Martin Luther, *Preface to the Psalter (1531)*, in *Works of Martin Luther* (Philadelphia: Holman and Castle, 1932), 6:385.

Day 6	Pss 18, 34, 103, 107, 118	Psalms of thanksgiving.
Day 7	Pss 16, 23, 46, 73, 139	Psalms of confidence in the Lord.

Consider...

- The Psalms cover the full range of human emotion and experience, including praise, protest, and lament. People of many generations have seen them as a word from God in time of need, speaking uniquely to their joy and suffering.
- Psalms are poetry. Many are poetic prayers. All were meant to be said aloud or chanted or sung. Hebrew poetry does not rhyme; rather, it often features parallel construction where the second line echoes the meaning of the first line using different words, or emphasizes the meaning of the first line by stating a contrast. Puns and other uses of wordplay are common, though usually hard to see in any translation.
- Some psalms have a definite structure; such as acrostics, in which each verse (Pss 9, 10, 25, 34, 37, 111, 112, 145) or each stanza (119) begins with successive letters of the twenty-two-character Hebrew alphabet.
- The terms *selah*, *miktam*, and *maskil* appear in some psalms. They appear to be directions for readers or musicians, but their meaning is lost.
- Have you heard modern attempts to put the psalms to music? How successful were they, do you think? Why did they succeed or fail?
- Monks and nuns in monasteries chant psalms several times a day. Many churches chant psalms weekly. Some hymnals include basic instructions for chanting. Check YouTube and other online sources for recordings, then try it. You might find it more spiritually uplifting than you expect.
- More than seventy psalms are said to be "of David." That may mean that he wrote them or that they appeared in a collection under his name or were dedicated to him.
- Which of your favorite psalms were on this week's reading list? Why do these especially speak to you? Do any psalms disturb or puzzle you?

- The so-called imprecatory psalms call on God to act against the writer's enemies. Some seek justice or revenge in general terms, including Pss 7, 55, 59, 70, 79, and 139. Others are sometimes graphically specific: 5:10; 10:15; 17:13–14; 35:4–8, 26; 58:6–9; 69:22–28; 83:13–17; 109:6–20; 137; and 140:10. One asks God to punish his enemies but not kill them (59:11). These psalms are definitely signs that it's OK to "let it all hang out" before God. But do they condone, even invite, bad behavior?

- Seven "penitential" psalms express sorrow for sins: Pss 6, 32, 38, 51, 102, 130, 143.

- Many pocket New Testaments include the Psalms at the end because the Psalms were the prayer book and hymnal of Israel. Some object that this practice leaves out the heart of the Hebrew Bible. What do you think? Do the Psalms summarize the rest well?

- Some pocket New Testaments also include the Proverbs. Are they as valuable as the Psalms? Does including them in the New Testament lend them too much value?

- The royal psalms were originally intended for use in the king's court and later got messianic interpretation. Among them are Pss 2, 20, 21, 44, 72, 93, 97, and 110.

- The Songs of Ascents are fifteen relatively short psalms, from Ps 120 to Ps 134. They were sung by worshipers as they ascended the road to Jerusalem or the Temple Mount during the pilgrim festivals of Pesach (Passover), Shavuot (Weeks), and Sukkot (Booths).

- In 1:5–6 and elsewhere, the psalmist seems to express the Deuteronomistic view that God always rewards the righteous and punishes the wicked. Or does it simply express faith in God's providence?

PART 6

Gospel

God Comes Down to Earth

OVER THE NEXT EIGHT weeks, we'll read large portions of the four "Gospels" that proclaim the "good news" (or "gospel") of Jesus. If you have never read these books so closely before, you may be amazed at the insights you pick up reading the story continuously.

Summary

Week 1, Messiah—God Becomes Human in Jesus

Week 2, Teacher—Jesus Shows the Way to Eternal Life

Week 3, Prophet—Jesus Reveals God's Mission

Week 4, Light—Jesus Reveals His Glory and Destiny

Week 5, Master—Jesus Reveals the Cost of Following Him

Week 6, Shepherd—Jesus Reveals More of the Kingdom

Week 7, Savior—Jesus Confronts His Enemies in Jerusalem

Week 8, Redeemer—Jesus Dies on the Cross and Is Resurrected

You've seen those WWJD signs or bracelets, asking you to consider "What would Jesus do?" when making a decision. To answer that question, of course, you need to know something about what Jesus *did*. That means you need to read the Gospels. For Christians, they are the heart of the Bible. They tell us how God acts in Jesus to show us personally what God is like and how God saves us. Why *four* accounts? As John suggests (21:25), the world cannot contain all the accounts that *could* be written.

1

Messiah

God Becomes Human in Jesus

THE GOSPELS OF *MATTHEW*, *Mark*, *Luke*, and *John* are evangelistic biographies of Jesus. Each is written for a different audience and tells the story from a different perspective, but they share a common purpose. They are intended to provide "an orderly account of the events that have been fulfilled among us" (Luke 1:1) so that "you may come to believe that Jesus is the Messiah, the Son of God, and that through believing you may have life in his name" (John 20:31).

> My soul magnifies the Lord,
> and my spirit rejoices in God my Savior,
> for he has looked with favor upon the lowliness of his servant.
> —Luke 1:47-48

Day 1	John 1:1–18	Jesus is the creative Word of God.
→ *Deeper*	Matt 1:1–17	Matthew gives a genealogy of Jesus.
→ *Deeper*	Luke 3:23–38	Luke gives a very different genealogy of Jesus.
Day 2	Luke 1:5–80	Jesus is conceived by the Spirit.
Day 3	Matt 1:18—2:23	Jesus is born in Bethlehem.
Day 4	Luke 2:1–40	Angels and others herald Jesus' birth.
→ *Deeper*	Luke 2:41–52	Here is a story of Jesus' youth.
Day 5	Matt 3:1—4:11	Jesus is baptized and tested by the devil.

PART 6: GOSPEL

| *Day 6* | John 1:29—2:11 | Jesus does his first "sign" at a wedding. |
| *Day 7* | John 3:1–36 | Jesus guides a religious leader. |

Consider...

- Read the luminous opening of John aloud. Does that make it more meaningful?
- The opening of John identifies the Word and the Son with God and with Jesus (though the name *Jesus* does not appear until 1:17). It must be noted that the eternal Word is a human being (1:14), the Son of God, the Living Word, not a book, as some seem to think.
- Trace *logos* ("word") from Prov 8:22 to John 1:14 to 1 Cor 1:24 to Heb 4:12. (For more on the Hebrews passage, see part 9, week 3, day 2.)
- You've heard stories of Jesus' birth many times at Christmas. Do any parts stand out for you this time—or have you heard it so often that it can't speak to you freshly?
- Matthew is eager to apply prophecies to Jesus—and he does it nearly fifty times, sometimes with little regard for the original sense of the text. For example, Isaiah says "the young woman is with child" (Isa 7:14). Matthew reads that as "the virgin shall conceive" (see Matt 1:23). No "virginal conception" was reported in Isaiah's time. How and why does Matthew reinterpret God's sign in Isaiah?
- If the birth of Jesus is such a big deal, why is it announced to shepherds and foreigners and two temple charismatics rather than to "important" people?
- Luke tells the story of Jesus' birth from Mary's point of view and Matthew from Joseph's. The two versions may reflect the traditions of their birth families. Differences in the two genealogies can't be explained. Though some have suggested that Matthew traces Joseph's family and Luke traces Mary's family, the texts report both lines as that of Joseph.
- If Jesus was conceived by the Holy Spirit, why do Matthew and Luke try so hard to show that his family's line goes back to David?
- It is possible to merge the two birth accounts into one continuous narrative, as Christmas pageants often do. Note, though, that the magi ("wise men") cannot appear until after the purification of

Mary, forty days after Jesus' birth. We push the chronology pretty hard when we celebrate the magi's visit at Epiphany, on January 6, only twelve days after Christmas.

- Luke's account of Jesus tempted in the wilderness (Luke 4:1–13) lists the same three temptations as Matthew (Matt 4:1–11), but the last two in different order. The story must have originated with Jesus himself, so one of the Gospel writers must have flipped the two temptations to emphasize one more than the other. Why would he do that in this case? Does this inconsistency in the accounts trouble you?

- When John uses the term "the Jews" (throughout John starting at 1:19), he mostly refers to Jewish leaders and other enemies of the Jesus movement, *not* Jewish people in general. His negative polemic reflects conflicts in his own day.

- The turning of water into wine at Cana is sometimes belittled as a minor thing, but John (2:1–11) stresses its importance as the first of Jesus' seven signs. It certainly must have been impressive to the few who were aware of it. Your reaction?

- John's Gospel is built around seven signs and seven "I am" statements that reveal aspects of Jesus' identity and mission. The signs are turning water into wine (2:1–11); healing an official's son (4:46–54); healing a paralyzed man (5:1–15); feeding five thousand and walking on water (6:1–21); healing a man born blind (9:1–7); and raising Lazarus from the grave (11:1–45). For the "I am" statements, see notes on week 4.

2

Teacher

Jesus Shows the Way to Eternal Life

ALL THE GOSPELS ARE anonymous. They are linked to figures from the apostolic age only by traditions that date from the second century. Mark probably was the first to be written because Matthew and Luke clearly rely on it. Together the three are called the "Synoptic" Gospels because they share a common outline, or synopsis, of the life of Jesus. The Fourth Gospel, John, comes from a different tradition altogether, and from ancient times has been thought to be the last one written. Scholars generally date the Gospels from 65–85 CE (or somewhat later for John).

> The time is fulfilled, and the kingdom of God has come near. Repent and believe in the good news. —Mark 1:15

Day 1	John 4:1–54	Jesus befriends a Samaritan woman.
Day 2	Mark 1:14–45	Jesus proclaims the kingdom's coming.
Day 3	Mark 2:1–28	Jesus is Lord of the Sabbath.
Day 4	Matt 5	Jesus pronounces God's blessings.
→ *Deeper*	Luke 6:17–49	. . . And some woes, too.
Day 5	Matt 6	Jesus teaches about prayer and ultimate value.
Day 6	Matt 7	Don't judge others, Jesus says.
Day 7	John 5:1–47	Jesus heals a paralyzed man.

Consider . . .

- Why does Jesus "have" to go through Samaria (John 4:4)? Couldn't he go another way?
- Why does Jesus spend so much time speaking with a life-worn woman of Samaria? Doesn't he know how many social taboos he is breaking?
- Why do some readers assume the worst about the woman at the well? What if she's the victim here, someone who's been divorced or widowed five times? Don't you find her a sympathetic character?
- In Mark chapter 2, notice how quickly opposition to Jesus rises, and over what issues. Also notice that challenges do not deter him.
- Why must new wine not be poured into old wineskins (Mark 2:22)?
- The clash between Jesus and the Pharisees over the Sabbath may stem from two versions of the commandment. Exodus 20:8–11 and Deut 5:13–15 both require Sabbath rest, but for different reasons. Do you see how that could play out? Compare John 5:16–17.
- The Sermon on the Mount (Matt 5–7) and the Sermon on the Plain (Luke 6:20–49) are compilations or summaries of Jesus' teaching, not verbatim accounts of two sermons. They announce "kingdom values." These are not new laws or lofty ethical standards that are impossible to keep. Rather, they describe ways we are *free* to act in Christ and are *expected* to act as followers of Christ now living in God's kingdom.
- Why do some activists want to post copies of the Ten Commandments everywhere, rather than the Beatitudes?
- What does it mean to be blessed? Do you consider yourself blessed?
- When the Beatitudes use the passive tense ("for they will be comforted"), who does the comforting?
- Compare the two versions of the Beatitudes. Why are they so similar and yet so different? Could they be meant for different audiences and different circumstances—for the Gospel writers and for Jesus?
- Compare the versions of the Lord's Prayer from Matt 6:9–13 and Luke 11:2–4. What are the chief differences and similarities? Again, why are there two versions?
- How can we be perfect as God is perfect (Matt 5:43–48)?

PART 6: GOSPEL

- Jesus never uses the word that is so often translated as "hell." In Matt 5:22 and elsewhere, he speaks of *Gehenna*, the Hinnom Valley. It was desecrated by human sacrifices during the reigns of apostate kings, so it was turned into a city dump where fires always burn and the worm never dies (Mark 9:48).

- Jesus' teaching on divorce (Matt 5:31–32, 19:3–12, Mark 10:2–12) is open to many interpretations. Consult commentaries you consider authoritative.

- The so-called Golden Rule (Matt 7:12 and Luke 6:31) is not unique to Jesus. It was taught by other first-century rabbis and has parallels in other religions.

- In Matthew, Jesus says that two rules sum up all God's ethical teaching: "Do to others as you would have them do to you" (7:12) and "Love the Lord your God with all your heart, and with all your soul and with all your mind . . . and love your neighbor as yourself" (22:37–40). Which of these two rules strike the strongest chord with you?

- For Jesus' teaching about the birds and wildflowers and true treasure, see week 5.

3

Prophet
Jesus Reveals God's Mission

MARK PROBABLY IS THE earliest Gospel, likely written for mostly gentile Christians in Rome. It may be the work of John Mark, a disciple of Paul and Barnabas and later also Peter, whose memories he likely preserves. Writing in a breathless style, Mark emphasizes the mystery of Jesus' identity and the difficult path of discipleship.

> The Spirit of the Lord is upon me,
> because he has anointed me to
> bring good news to the poor.
> He has sent me to proclaim release to the captives
> and recovery of sight to the blind,
> to let the oppressed go free,
> to proclaim the year of the Lord's favor.
> —Luke 4:18–19

Day 1	Mark 3:1–35	Jesus names an inner circle of followers.
Day 2	Mark 4:1–41	Jesus describes the kingdom in parables.
Day 3	Mark 5:1–43	Here are tales of wonder.
Day 4	Luke 4:16–30	Jesus is rejected at home.
Day 5	Matt 10:1–42	Jesus sends out the Twelve.
Day 6	Matt 11:2–30	Jesus reassures John.
Day 7	Luke 7:1–17, 36–50	Here are more signs of faith and new life.

Consider...

- A *disciple* is a learner, a student, or pupil of the teacher or master. An *apostle* is one who is sent out as a special representative. The terms are used inconsistently in the New Testament to mean the twelve disciples/apostles or other missionaries such as Paul. Are you a disciple or an apostle or both?

- Mark often "sandwiches" stories to show connections between them. Find examples of a "Markan sandwich" in Mark 3, 5, 6, 11, and 14. (And you thought this was a modern storytelling technique!)

- Blasphemy against the Holy Spirit (Mark 3:29) is willful, continual denial of God's working in the world, so it has eternal consequences. Can you see such activity in the world today?

- What's the issue in the parable of the sower (Mark 4:2–8, 13–20)? Why does God throw seed around so indiscriminately? What determines whether it will grow? Have you seen how this works in yourself and others?

- The "secret of the kingdom" (Mark 4:11) is dawning in Jesus. It's "secret" because people can't clearly see it happening. Later, in Paul's letters, the "secret" may be described as a "mystery" (the same word in Greek). See, for example, 1 Cor 2:7–8, Eph 3:3–5, and Col 1:26. How does this secret "get out"?

- Jesus teaches as his listeners are able to hear (Mark 4:33). Are you sometimes surprised at what truths you are able to hear now that you couldn't earlier? What does this tell you about the process of maturing in faith?

- Jesus' parables are not just cutesy folk tales. Jesus is challenging his listeners to think and maybe to be changed by an unexpected insight into the way God works. Yet he may also suggest that parables are intended to conceal the message from some people (Mark 4:11–14, referring to Isa 6:9–10; see parallels in Matt 13:12–14 and Luke 8:10). Commentators are divided. Do you think hiding the message is really Jesus' intent? Or is he saying that some people just won't get it?

- Why doesn't Jesus want the man he freed from demons to follow him (Mark 5:1–20)?

- Have you ever felt buffeted by conflicting forces pulling you in many directions?
- Why can't Jesus do great things in his hometown (Mark 6:5–6)? It's said, "You can't go home again." Have you ever felt uncomfortable returning home? Why is Jesus rejected so sharply?
- Prophets are rejected not only in their hometowns but also by their own kin. They later support him, but early in his ministry members of Jesus' own family think he has lost his mind (Mark 3:21). Some scribes from Jerusalem go further; they say he's possessed by an unclean spirit (3:30). So you want to be a prophet, do you?
- Why does John the Baptizer ask Jesus, "Are you the one?" (Matt 11:3)? To what messianic themes do Jesus' answers refer?
- All four Gospels tell a story about a woman anointing Jesus at a dinner, but two incidents are involved. In Luke 7:36–50, the event occurs early in Jesus' ministry, at a dinner given by Simon the Pharisee. The woman is called a "sinner," and Jesus says her sins are forgiven. The other anointing occurs in Bethany shortly before Jesus' death. It may, in fact, trigger the betrayal by Judas. Versions of this story are narrated in Mark 14:3–9, Matt 26:6–13, and John 12:1–8. Mark and Matthew identify the host as Simon the Leper, and John identifies the woman as Mary, a sister of Lazarus. Despite similarities, the two stories are different.

4

Light
Jesus Reveals His Glory and Destiny

THE GOSPEL OF MATTHEW was written for Jewish Christians, probably those in Antioch of Syria. The Gospel expands Mark's account with several stories that are unique to it, plus many sayings of Jesus that also appear in the Gospel of Luke. Tradition links this Gospel to the apostle Matthew, who reportedly collected the sayings of Jesus in their original tongue (probably Aramaic). This "sayings" document possibly underlies both Matthew and Luke, but Matthew's Gospel as we have it likely is the work of another hand. Structured around five discourses to match the five-part Torah, the Gospel portrays Jesus as the fulfillment of Israel's hope and a "new Moses" for a new age.

> I am the light of the world. Whoever follows me will never walk in darkness but will have the light of life. —John 8:12

Day 1	Matt 14:1–33	Jesus feeds five thousand, walks on water.
Day 2	John 6:22–71	I am the bread of life.
Day 3	Mark 7:1–37	Jesus attacks religious traditions.
Day 4	Mark 8:1—9:1	Who do you say I am?
Day 5	Mark 9:2–50	Jesus reveals his true glory.
Day 6	John 7:1–53	Jesus' teaching astonishes and repels.
Day 7	John 8:1–59	Jesus antagonizes still more people.

Consider...

- Peter's confession (Mark 8:27-33) is the turning point in Mark's story. Now every movement leads Jesus toward the cross.
- Why is it so important for Jesus to know who his disciples think he is?
- Why does Jesus tell his disciples not to tell anyone else who he is?
- Why is Jesus so angry when Peter tries to correct him?
- Why is it significant that the transfiguration occurs six days after Jesus first speaks of his coming suffering?
- What does the transfiguration reveal to the three disciples who witness it?
- Pharisees added so many rules to ritual hand washing that it was too burdensome for many people (Mark 7:1-8). Can you think of practices that Christian religious leaders have similarly blown out of proportion?
- Are you shocked by Jesus' initial reaction to the Syrophoenician woman's request (Mark 7:24-30)? Does the spunk of her reaction please you as much as it apparently does Jesus? Or was he deliberately baiting her all along?
- Jesus refers to himself as "Son of Man" (*ben adam* or "Son of Adam") nearly eighty times in the Gospels. The enigmatic title has several layers of meaning. It can be simply a colorful way of referring to yourself in the third person. From its use in Ezekiel, it carries the connotation of "mere mortal." In Dan 7:13-14, it suggests a special representative of God who will usher in God's kingdom. Jesus may adopt the elusive identity because it's a lot safer than just blurting out, "I am the Messiah."
- The Common English Bible often replaces "Son of Man" with "the Human One." What's good or not so good about this rendering, in your opinion? Might "the True Human" be better?
- When Jesus tells people to take up their cross and follow him (Mark 8:34-35), he is pointing to the high cost of discipleship. How high is the cost for you?
- The story of the woman caught in adultery, related in John 8:1-11, is not in some early manuscripts of John, and in some later manuscripts

it is placed elsewhere in John, or even in Luke. But the story seems so characteristic of Jesus that few commentators dispute its authenticity. Is it just "too much like Jesus" to lose?

- Where's her partner? Although the woman is said to have been caught in the act of adultery, her partner is not accused. According to Lev 20:10 and Deut 22:22, both probably should have been. Why would charging them both be less useful for Jesus' opponents?

- Many commentators speculate on what Jesus writes on the ground. More likely, he is just scribbling to gain time—time to think about his response and time to defuse the situation by throwing his confident accusers off guard.

- Two of the seven traditional "I am" statements are included in this week's readings: "I am the bread of life" (John 6:35), and "I am the light of the world" (8:12). Others are "I am the gate" (10:7); "I am the good shepherd" (10:11); "I am the resurrection and the life" (11:25); "I am the way, the truth, and the life" (14:6); and "I am the true vine" (15:1). Jesus also says that "I am" the Messiah (4:26); one sent from God (7:29); from above and not of this world (8:23); from the Father (8:19); God's Son (10:36); teacher and lord (13:13); and a king (18:37).

5

Master

Jesus Reveals the Cost of Following Him

THE GOSPEL OF LUKE was written perhaps primarily for gentile Christians, probably by the physician Luke, who accompanied Paul on his missionary journeys. Luke says he compiled his story from many sources (Luke 1:1–3). These include the Gospel of Mark and the same "sayings" source used by Matthew. Luke also reports many stories that are unique to him. Luke's Gospel and the book of Acts form a two-part work. The most elegantly written of the Gospels, Luke stresses the humanity of Jesus, his fulfillment of God's promises, and God's concern for social justice.

> Whoever does not carry the cross and follow me cannot be my disciple. —Luke 14:27

Day 1	John 9:1–41	Jesus heals a man born blind.
Day 2	John 10:1–21	I am the good shepherd, Jesus says.
	Luke 9:51–62	Jesus begins his final tour of ministry.
Day 3	Luke 10:1–42	Jesus sends out seventy to prepare the way.
Day 4	Luke 11:5–54	Don't expect signs, Jesus says.
Day 5	Luke 12:1–59	Keep your lamps lit.
Day 6	Luke 13:1–35	Strive to enter the narrow door.
Day 7	Luke 14:1–35	Count the cost of discipleship.

PART 6: GOSPEL

Consider...

- Like the Pharisees who persecute the man born blind (John 9), religious officials can be spiritually blind. Any modern parallels you care to name?

- What do the Pharisees ignore while tithing their garden herbs (Luke 11:42)? Have you ever been so hung up on minor things that you missed the big thing?

- Psalm 80:1, Isa 40:11, and other passages praise God as the shepherd of Israel, so Jesus is making no small claim when he says, "I am the good shepherd" (John 10:11). Though most of us today probably know little about herding sheep, the "good shepherd" metaphor speaks to many of us deeply. How about you? Why or why not?

- In Luke, the turning point in Jesus' ministry occurs at 9:51, when Jesus "set his face to go to Jerusalem." Much of the material from 9:51 to 18:14 is unique to Luke, as Jesus uses this time to prepare his disciples for what is to come. Does knowing the context help you understand the gravity of what's happening and Jesus' approach to it?

- In Luke's story of Mary and Martha (10:38–42), don't we often denigrate Martha? Isn't she serving Jesus as well as Mary? Can't she be listening even while she's working? What's the "one thing" that Jesus says Martha is missing in her quarrel with Mary?

- Jesus often speaks in hyperbole. Does this amplify or confuse his point? Does he really mean that disciples must hate their families (Luke 14:26) or that they must put him first? Similarly, what does "give up all your possessions" mean (Luke 14:33)?

- Is the point of Jesus' story in Luke 11:5–13 that we ought to badger God in prayer the way this guy badgers his friend in the middle of the night? Or is there something else about persistence in prayer that's important here? See Luke 18:1–7 for a similar story with a similar point.

- "Don't worry," Jesus says (Luke 12:22). Isn't this sometimes very hard?

- "Consider the birds and wildflowers," Jesus says (Luke 12:22–34, Matt 6:25–34). Why is it significant that he offers these common parts of creation?

MASTER

- How does seeking God's kingdom first (Luke 12:31, Matt 6:33) put our priorities in proper order? Is this the "one thing" Martha had out of order?

- "Give it another year," the vinedresser asks the vineyard owner, so the unfruitful tree is spared the axe (Luke 13:6–9). Ever felt like that tree, grateful for a little more time to get your act together and maybe some extra attention, too (even if it may feel like dung at the time)?

- The incidents of the Galileans slain by Pilate and the Judeans who die when the tower of Siloam falls on them are unknown outside of Luke 13:1–5. As in John 9:3, Jesus denies that disease or calamity is punishment for sin. Why do so many Christians today insist that God "punishes" the wicked in these ways, especially when others suffer as collateral damage?

- Jesus can be a less-than-desirable dinner guest. In Luke 14:1–14, he lectures his host and other guests about proper seating arrangements. In 7:36–50, he lectures his host about other aspects of dinner etiquette. Of course, both occasions are a setup by his enemies who are hoping to trap him in some way.

- "Be dressed for action and have your lamps lit," Jesus says in Luke 12:35. Similar stories in Mark 13:33–37 and in the parable of the ten bridesmaids in Matt 25:1–13 make the same point: "Keep alert" and "Stay awake." But how can you keep constantly awake and alert?

6

Shepherd

Jesus Reveals More of the Kingdom

THE GOSPEL OF JOHN is markedly different from the Synoptic Gospels in chronology, style, and interpretative emphasis. The story is built around the eyewitness testimony of "the beloved disciple," whom tradition identifies as the apostle John. It was written for a community of Jewish converts who were in sharp conflict with other Jews—hence, its harsh condemnation of its estranged brethren, "the Jews." The Gospel stresses Jesus' proclamation of the fatherhood of God and his divine relation to God.

> The kingdom of God is not coming with things that can be observed; nor will they say, "Look, here it is!" or "There it is!" For, in fact, the kingdom of God is among you. —Luke 17:20–21

Day 1	Luke 15:1–32	The shepherd seeks the lost sheep.
Day 2	Luke 16:1–31	No one can serve two masters.
Day 3	Luke 17:1–37	The kingdom offers true security.
Day 4	Matt 13:24–30, 36–53	It's like weeds and wheat.
	Luke 18:1–14	Be persistent in your requests.
Day 5	Matt 18:15–35	How forgiving should I be?
	Matt 20:1–16	God is generous beyond understanding.
Day 6	Matt 25:1–46	Keep awake and ready.
Day 7	Mark 10:1–52	It's not easy for some to get in.

Consider...

- Many of the stories Jesus tells in this week's readings involve money and relationships. What's the connection? Jesus talks about money a lot. When we say, "Money isn't important," aren't we lying to ourselves?
- Ever lost something so important that you turned your house inside out to find it? If you finally found it, how did that make you feel?
- Do you think the shepherd abandons the ninety-nine sheep to seek the lost one (Luke 15:3–7)? Should those "left behind" feel resentful of the one who strayed? Don't we often celebrate those who remain faithful more than those who stray and return?
- What's at stake in the story of the prodigal son (Luke 15:11–32)? Aren't *both* brothers prodigals? Isn't this really a story about a loving father and his two wayward sons? Have you ever behaved like one or the other brothers? Have you ever felt forgiven? Why is this parable among Jesus' most important as well as his most famous?
- It's hard to understand the point of the parable of the dishonest steward (Luke 16:1–9). Check commentaries to see the many interpretations.
- If you farm or garden, you know how persistent and annoying weeds are. Why does Jesus say we can ignore them in our midst (Matt 13:24–30, 36–50)? Why do we so desire to root out the weeds in our midst? Why should we let the judgment ultimately rest with God alone?
- In the parable of the unforgiving servant (Matt 18:21–35), the servant owes an impossibly large amount but is unforgiving to someone who owes a lot less. Ever caught yourself dealing with others that way?
- How often should we forgive someone? At least seventy-seven times, Jesus says in Matt 18:22. (For the possible significance of seventy-seven, see the story of Lamech's vengeance in Gen 4:24.) A variant reading of Matthew says "seven times seventy." Either way, could you realistically keep track of so many offenses? And if you're counting so carefully, aren't you missing the point entirely?
- The "seventy-seven" saying has been used to keep women captive in abusive situations. Can you see how evil that is?
- Don't look for signs of the coming kingdom, Jesus says; just look around you (Luke 17:20–21). Where is the kingdom? Can you see it?

- The parable of the workers in the vineyard (Matt 20:1–16) suggests that God is generous but not necessarily "fair." How does that sit with you? We're taught since childhood to always be fair, but is fairness the highest standard we should strive for?
- Jesus' acceptance of children (Mark 10:13–16 and elsewhere) is notable in a time when children don't count for much socially. Despite all our sentimentality and heated rhetoric, do we really value children much higher today?
- The "eye of a needle" saying (Mark 10:25, Matt 19:24, Luke 18:25) is obviously hyperbole. What's the point of it?
- Some commentators want to soften the hyperbole. The Greek words for "rope" and "camel" are easily confused, so it's possible that Jesus means, "It is easier for a rope to go through the eye of a needle." Either way, it's not going to happen!
- It's also been claimed that the "needle's eye" was a small gate in the walls of Jerusalem that was closed at night, and a camel could not get through without shedding its load. It's a clever story about the importance of shedding attachment to possessions. But there is no evidence that such a gate existed in Jesus' day.

7

Savior

Jesus Confronts His Enemies in Jerusalem

> I am the resurrection and the life. Those who believe in me, even though they die, will live, and everyone who lives and believes in me will never die. —John 11:25–26

Day 1	Luke 19:1–10	A crooked tax collector repents.
	John 10:22–42	Jesus escapes arrest by his enemies.
Day 2	John 11:1–44	Jesus raises Lazarus from the dead.
Day 3	John 11:45–57	The authorities conspire against Jesus.
Day 4	Mark 11:1–33	Jesus enters Jerusalem in triumph.
Day 5	Mark 12:1–44	Jesus teaches in the temple.
Day 6	Matt 23:1–36	Jesus denounces religious leaders.
Day 7	Mark 13:1–37	Jesus warns of a great trial coming.
→ *Deeper*	John 12:20–50	Jesus comes not to judge but to save.

Consider...

- The rich man of Mark 10:17–22 is unwilling to part with all his wealth. Zacchaeus (Luke 19:1–10) gives away half of his wealth to show his change of heart. Why doesn't Jesus ask for more? What's really at stake in both stories?

- John 10 and 11 show Jesus acting carefully to avoid arrest. After a heated confrontation with his enemies at the Feast of Dedication

PART 6: GOSPEL

(10:22–39), he retreats to the desert. He appears in public again only after Lazarus dies but then immediately returns to the desert while his enemies plot against him (11:45–57). People wonder, Will he dare show his face in Jerusalem at Passover?

- The story of Jesus raising Lazarus (John 11:1–44) is one of the most dramatic in Scripture. Try reading it in a group, with assigned parts, to get a better feel for it.
- Jesus knows that he will raise Lazarus from the dead, but he still weeps. Why?
- By riding a donkey into Jerusalem (Mark 11:1–10), Jesus announces that he is Messiah (see Zech 9:9). He demonstrates his authority by "cleansing" the temple. Do temple officials need any more provocation to arrest him?
- *Hosanna* means "Save us!" (see Ps 118:25–26). From what or from whom do the people want saving? Who will save them?
- The parable of the murderous tenants (Mark 12:1–12) is so obviously aimed at the religious leaders that even *they* get it, but it does not deter them from acting against Jesus. Is it a trait of the powerful that they should be so shameless?
- If you love the Lord with all your heart and soul and mind and strength (Mark 12:30), is any part of you left to serve Caesar? What is Caesar "due"?
- Do you see in Mark 12:33 the danger that Jesus' teaching poses to the religious authorities? No wonder they stop asking him questions!
- In Matt 23:8–10, Jesus warns against the use of honorific titles in the faith community. He does not appear concerned about using the word *father* to describe a parent but about giving undue honor to human spiritual mentors. Still, priests and monks have been called *father* (and female mentors *mother*) since the early days of Christianity. Is this any more harmful than calling someone *pastor* or *elder*?
- Jesus "curses" the fig tree for appearing to bear fruit when it has not (Mark 11:13–14, 20–21). Mark sandwiches the story around Jesus' attack on temple authorities, who are as deceptive as the fig tree. The "lesson of the fig tree," Jesus later says (13:28), is being alert to signs of the times. He's talking about the destruction of Jerusalem and his

"coming in the clouds"—both of which will happen while "this generation" lives (13:30), though even he doesn't know exactly when (13:32).

- Mark 13 (and parallels in Matt 24 and Luke 21) is often called the "Little Apocalypse" because some commentators think it predicts the "end times." It doesn't. Jesus is talking about the end of "the age," not the end of the world.

- The "seven woes" of Matt 23:13–36 are Jesus' strongest and most sustained attack on the religious leaders of his day. Calling them "whitewashed tombs" refers to the practice of painting tombs white, partly out of respect for the dead and partly to keep the living from accidentally coming into contact with them and becoming ritually unclean. Do you know any whitewashed tombs you should avoid?

8

Redeemer

Jesus Dies on the Cross and Is Resurrected

> Why do you seek the living among the dead? He is not here, but has risen. —Luke 24:5

Day 1	Mark 14:1–25	Jesus shares a final meal with his disciples.
	John 13:1–30	Before the meal, Jesus washes his disciple's feet.
Day 2	John 13:31—14:31	Jesus gives a new commandment.
	John 17:1–26	Jesus prays for his disciples.
Day 3	Mark 14:32–72	Jesus is betrayed and arrested.
	Matt 27:3–10	Judas repents and hangs himself.
Day 4	BIG DAY	*Good Friday*
	Mark 15:1–20	Jesus is tried and condemned to die.
	Luke 23:4–12	Herod mocks Jesus.
	Luke 23:26–43	Jesus is crucified between two criminals.
	Mark 15:33–47	Jesus cries out in agony and dies.
Day 5	BIG DAY	*Easter morning*
	Matt 27:62—28:15, Mark 16:1–8, Luke 24:1–12, John 20:1–18	
Day 6	Luke 24:13–49	Jesus appears to two followers on the road.

Day 7	John 20:19—21:19	Jesus appears to his disciples.
	Matt 28:16–20	Jesus commissions his disciples.

Consider...

- When the Gospel of John refers to "the Jews," it usually means only those who are enemies of Jesus. In John 20:19, for example, the disciples hide "for fear of the Jews." They don't fear themselves, surely! Such passages have fueled many generations of anti-Semitism, but they have to be read as signs of a bitter squabble within the Jewish family that gave birth to Christ and to Christianity.

- Why does Judas betray Jesus? What does Judas expect to happen next? Luke 22:3 and John 13:27 may provide the best explanation ("Satan entered" him), but that still leaves his motive unclear. What's your take?

- The religious authorities find Jesus guilty of blasphemy—a crime punishable by stoning (Lev 24:16). So why don't they stone him? (See John 18:31.)

- Crucifixion was a punishment so ghastly that Romans reserved it for slaves and rebels. They rarely spoke of it in public, though they killed untold thousands this way. Why does Jesus have to die in such a horrible manner? Couldn't his death have saving value without him suffering so much?

- Barabbas is a "notorious" insurrectionist (Matt 27:16, Mark 15:7, Luke 23:19). John calls him a "bandit" (John 18:40), a euphemism for rebels. The two "bandits" executed with Jesus were arrested with Barabbas (Mark 15:7). Does it bother you that Jesus died not among "thieves" but among rebels and insurgents?

- How is Jesus' cry of despair (Mark 15:34) also a cry a hope? (See Ps 22.)

- Why are there only women at the cross except for the "beloved disciple"?

- Why are the initial resurrection announcements made only to women?

- Does it bother you that the four resurrection stories differ in detail? Why or why not? Is reconciling the differences possible? Do we need to even try? Aren't eyewitness accounts often at odds with one another?

PART 6: GOSPEL

- By accident or intent, Mark 16 ends at verse 8. Does this seem like an appropriate ending to you? If the original ending has been lost, why would God allow such a thing, if every word of Scripture is sacred?

- Mark's odd ending isn't the only one in the Gospels. John has *two* endings—chapter 20 and chapter 21. The latter has the feeling of an "oops, I forgot" addition. But wouldn't it be a great loss if we didn't have it?

- John's "second ending" (ch. 21) involves a huge catch of fish. Does this remind you of another episode in the Gospels? (See Luke 5:1–11.)

- Cleopas is one of the two followers Jesus meets on the road to Emmaus (Luke 24:13–35). The other one is not named. Because they apparently live together (24:29), the unnamed disciple is probably his wife. Women often go unnamed in the Gospels. Can you name other women who never get a name despite a prominent role in a Gospel story?

- Why isn't Jesus immediately recognizable after his resurrection? Does this suggest anything about our recognition of Jesus' presence in our lives?

- John's Gospel never clearly reveals the identity of the "beloved disciple" who first appears at the Last Supper. He is traditionally thought to be John, son of Zebedee, but some commentators think he is not one of the Twelve. At any rate, there is hint of a rivalry between him and Simon Peter that appears in 20:3–10 and 21:20–23. Can you call yourself a "beloved disciple"?

PART 7

Witness

Jesus' Teaching Spreads Widely

OVER THE NEXT THREE weeks, we'll follow the Jesus movement from its early days in Jerusalem to its establishment in the capital of the Roman Empire. The author of Luke's Gospel also wrote the book of Acts. Both books are addressed to Theophilus, meaning "God lover." The name could be a real person or a symbolic figure.

Summary

Week 1, Anointing—Disciples Are Filled with the Holy Spirit

Week 2, Expansion—Mission to the Gentiles Causes Conflict

Week 3, Trials—Paul's Enemies Can't Silence Him

In the second part of his account of Christian origins, the author of the Gospel of Luke provides a broad survey of early church history, concentrating on the ministries of Peter and—especially—Paul. The chronology of Acts is occasionally precise but more often quite vague (as in 9:23, when Luke uses the phrase "some time" to describe what Paul elsewhere says is a period of three years). Even relative time markers are hard to match with the letters of Paul. (Acts never mentions Paul writing anything to anybody!) Though sometimes offering what appears to be an idealized portrait of the early church, Acts can be frank in its portrayal of conflict and the reasons for it. Both Paul and Peter die for their faith, but their deaths are not mentioned in Acts, and the dates and circumstances are not firmly established.

1

Anointing

Disciples Are Filled with the Holy Spirit

In the *Acts of the Apostles*, the writer of the Gospel of Luke continues his story by relating the work of the Holy Spirit in the early life of the church. Luke strives to show how God's promises are fulfilled in the life and mission of the church just as they were in the life and mission of Jesus and how it was always God's plan to expand this mission to gentiles. The "we" passages in chapters 16, 20, 21, and 27 may come from Luke's travel diary.

> Repent and be baptized, every one of you, in the name of Jesus Christ, so that your sins may be forgiven, and you will receive the gift of the Holy Spirit. —Acts 2:38

Day 1	Acts 1	Jesus ascends to heaven.
Day 2	Acts 2	At Pentecost, the Holy Spirit comes down.
Day 3	Acts 3:1—4:22	Bold proclaimers clash with the authorities.
Day 4	Acts 4:32—5:42	The church sees signs and warnings.
Day 5	Acts 6:1—7:53	A believer named Stephen faces charges.
Day 6	Acts 7:54—8:40	Stephen is killed and the church scattered.
Day 7	Acts 9	Saul encounters Christ on the road.

PART 7: WITNESS

Consider...

- Matthias is chosen by lot to fill the vacancy in the ranks of the Twelve (1:21–26). It's the last time the Bible mentions lots being used in decision making. Do you think it's a good way of making choices? If it's "biblical," why don't we do it today?

- Pentecost is also known as the Feast of Weeks because it comes seven weeks after Passover. It's also called the Feast of First Fruits because it originated as a celebration of the spring wheat festival. Passover, Pentecost, and the Feast of Booths (or Tabernacles) are the three pilgrimage festivals where a journey to Jerusalem was once expected. Because it falls in the same month that the law was given to Moses on Mount Sinai, Pentecost also is known as the time when God speaks—an appropriate designation for God speaking in a new way.

- How is Peter's Pentecost message similar to the early messages of John the Baptizer and Jesus? How has the church's message changed since then?

- What happens at Pentecost? Luke is obviously grasping for words to describe the event. Can you tell the story using different images? Have you seen signs of the Holy Spirit's power in your life? Are any of these signs easy to describe?

- The first division in the church is between those who speak Aramaic and those who speak Greek. It's apparently an ethnic thing rather than simply racial. Does it portend bigger divides ahead over more difficult issues?

- So what's wrong with church leaders waiting tables (6:2)?

- The seven who are chosen to serve are often regarded as the first "deacons" of the church—the title deriving from the Greek word for "servant." They also may have been the first "elders" or "presbyters." The creation and evolution of these roles in the early church is hard to reconstruct. Does confusion over them still exist today?

- Peter and John are examined by the same crowd that condemned Jesus (4:1–6). Why do they get off with just a warning? How does their community react when they are released (4:23–31)? What happens the next time they're arrested (5:17–42)?

- Gamaliel is a famous Pharisee teacher who was one of Saul's mentors. What might have happened if the authorities had followed his advice (Acts 5:34–39)?
- The early Christian community in Jerusalem practices a form of communalism in which most property is commonly held (2:44–45, 4:32). Does the story of Ananias and Sapphira (5:1–11) suggest how much strain this practice produces, and why it's soon abandoned?
- Stephen's witness is forceful. Can you see why council members are furious?
- How does the persecution that follows Stephen's death help spread the gospel (8:1)? Why does the persecution end abruptly with the conversion of Saul (9:31)?
- The Phillip who preaches in Samaria (8:5) and teaches the Ethiopian eunuch (8:26–40) is not one of the Twelve but one of the seven "deacons." Why do the Twelve stay in Jerusalem while others scatter to avoid persecution (8:1)?
- From what to what is Saul "converted"? He's still proud to say he's Jewish, though now he's a Jesus follower, too. Is he converted to a new way of being Jewish? Or to a new way of living? Is it even correct to say that he's "converted" at all?
- Read Acts 9:36–42, the story of Tabitha/Dorcas, in light of Mark 5:41. Do you think Peter echoes Jesus' words by saying, "Tabitha, koum," instead of "Talitha, koum"?

2

Expansion
Mission to the Gentiles Causes Conflict

> I truly understand that God shows no partiality, but in every nation anyone who fears him and does what is right is acceptable to him. —Acts 10:34–35

Day 1	Acts 10	Peter preaches to gentiles.
Day 2	Acts 11:1—12:19	The new outreach finds acceptance.
Day 3	Acts 13	Barnabas and Paul go on the road.
Day 4	Acts 14	Success means increasing opposition.
Day 5	Acts 15:1–35	The Jerusalem Council must decide.
Day 6	Acts 15:36—16:40	Paul and Barnabas split.
Day 7	Acts 17	Paul puzzles sophisticated Athenians.

Consider...

- The name *Barnabas* means "son of encouragement" or "one who encourages" (Acts 4:36). Do you have a Barnabas in your life? Are you an encourager to others?
- Act out the story of Peter and Rhoda (12:12–17). Isn't it hilariously true to life?
- What happens to the guards who allow Peter to escape (12:19)?
- According to Mark 7:19, Jesus declared all foods clean. Peter apparently didn't get it because he is initially horrified when he's ordered to

EXPANSION

"kill and eat." Still, he is willing to eat with Cornelius and other gentiles, and he sturdily defends his decision when confronted over it in Jerusalem (Acts 10–11). Later, though, Paul accuses him of hypocrisy on the issue (Gal 2:11–14). Why won't this question go away? What's so important about what you eat and who you eat with?

- What's really the central issue at the Jerusalem Council meeting (15:1–35)? How is this summit a turning point in the church's expansion?

- James the brother of Jesus is the council chair. He declares that the decision "seemed good to the Holy Spirit and to us" (15:28). Can we say that of all the decisions we make in the church? What does this suggest about how we make decisions? Or is casting lots a better idea?

- Why do Paul and Barnabas split over John Mark (15:36–41)? Is Paul being fair?

- John Mark later becomes a valued associate of Peter (1 Pet 5:13) and eventually of Paul, too (Col 4:10, Phlm 24, and especially 2 Tim 4:11). Do you wonder what he does to redeem himself with Paul? Does his reunion with Paul say anything about the possibility of reconciliation after church conflicts today?

- Paul calls Peter a hypocrite when Peter follows Jewish custom, but Paul has his own problem with hypocrisy. Timothy is the son of a Jewish woman and a Greek man. Though Jewish by birth, he was never circumcised. Paul has him circumcised to avoid giving offense to potential Jewish converts (16:1–4).

- Some gentiles are called "God-fearing" or "God fearer." They worship in the synagogue but do not accept circumcision or the restrictions of Jewish dietary and ritual law. These include Cornelius (10:1–2), Lydia (16:14), and others (13:26, 17:4). Paul may be especially despised by Jewish leaders because he targets God-fearers in their synagogues. Today we might call this practice "sheep stealing."

- Athenian philosophers think Paul is a hick (17:18). How does he fare before them?

- It appears to be common to be known by two names, one Jewish and one gentile, so it's telling that Saul becomes Paul (13:9) and John becomes Mark (12:12). The change does not signal a change in relationship with God, as in the Old Testament, but a change in how the person is perceived in the emerging church culture.

- Note that those who follow "the Way" (9:2) become "Christians" among gentiles (11:26) but are "Nazarenes" among Jews (24:5).
- The description "the sect of the Nazarenes" (24:5) suggests that Jews still consider Christians a sect within Judaism and thus subject to its rules. Do you see why they are so opposed to Paul's gospel of freedom from these rules?
- Freedom from ritual law seems so obvious to us today, but do you see how radically challenging it must have been to Jews when they, or their friends or family, started to follow Jesus?

3

Trials

Paul's Enemies Can't Silence Him

Although Acts never mentions them, Paul begins writing his letters during this period—first to the Thessalonians and Galatians and later to the Corinthians and others. Scholars generally agree on the order in which the books were written, but there is less consensus about when they were written and from where. For instance, were the "prison letters" (Philippians, Philemon, Colossians, and Ephesians) written from a jail in Ephesus, Caesarea, or Rome?

> I do not count my life of any value to myself, if only I may finish my course and the ministry that I received from the Lord Jesus, to testify to the good news of God's grace. —Acts 20:24

Day 1	Acts 18:1—19:10	Paul works in Corinth and Ephesus.
Day 2	Acts 19:21—20:6	Paul sets his sights on Rome.
Day 3	Acts 20:7—21:16	It's a farewell journey.
Day 4	Acts 21:17—22:29	In Jerusalem, Paul meets defeat.
Day 5	Acts 22:30—24:27	Roman justice moves slowly.
Day 6	Acts 25–26	Paul appeals to the emperor.
Day 7	Acts 27–28	A perilous journey brings Paul to Rome.

PART 7: WITNESS

Consider...

- What does the story of Apollos (18:24—19:6) tell you about diversity in the theology and practice of the early church? How and why are he and Paul considered rivals?

- What's the difference between the baptism of John and the baptism of Jesus (see 18:25, 19:1–7)? The baptism of John was for repentance and the forgiveness of sins (Mark 1:4, Acts 19:4). The baptism of Jesus is more contentious ground. From 8:14–17 and 19:5–6, we may say that it means baptism "in the name of Lord Jesus," with the laying on of hands and receiving the Holy Spirit. Prophetic or ecstatic speech may follow, though Acts does not mention these in all cases. What about Jesus' instruction (Matt 28:19) to baptize "in the name of the Father and of the Son and of the Holy Spirit"? The battle rages on today.

- What do the stories of Priscilla tell you about the role of women in Paul's ministry? Are you surprised to see him working side by side with a woman? How does his behavior here contrast with some of his more famous condemnations of women in ministry? Is Paul being inconsistent, or do we often misread him in light of our own cultural preferences?

- How does Paul cleverly play the Pharisees against the Sadducees (23:6–10)?

- How does Paul use his citizenship to gain advantage in several situations?

- Why don't leaders of the Jerusalem church defend Paul against Jewish leaders? After he risks his life bringing them a financial gift, wouldn't you expect at least some modest support from them? Why are they invisible and silent?

- Cast notes: The King Herod of Acts 12 is Herod Agrippa I, who ruled from 41 to 44 CE and ordered the execution of the apostle James and the arrest of Peter. The King Agrippa of Acts 25:13 is Herod Agrippa II, son of Agrippa I. Bernice is his sister and also his lover (though she's married to someone else). Drusilla (24:24) is a sister of Agrippa II and daughter of Agrippa I; she is the wife of Antonius Felix, the Roman governor of Judea from 52 to 60 CE. Happily, these are the last of the line of Herod the Great.

TRIALS

- King Agrippa says Paul could have been set free if he had not appealed to the emperor (26:32). Do you think Paul had any other choice (25:10)? Could he have gotten a fair trial in any Jewish court? (For a hint, see Acts 22:30—23:10.)
- Describe the role Paul plays in keeping the ship safe during the storm (27:13–44).
- Emperor Claudius expelled Jews from Rome about 50 CE (Acts 18:2), apparently because preaching about Jesus had caused an uproar among them. By the time Paul arrives in Rome, Claudius has died and many Jews have returned. Paul immediately seeks a meeting with Jewish leaders to head off new discord (28:17–28). How does it go?
- While awaiting trial in Rome, Paul lives under house arrest, apparently chained to a guard (28:16, 20). He has to foot the bill for his incarceration (28:30), but he is allowed to meet with people and preach unhindered. It takes a long time for his case to move through the bureaucracy, and he apparently makes good use of his time.
- Although written after Paul's death, the book of Acts ends with Paul awaiting trial. Luke is not telling the story of Paul but the story of the church, which has now spread the gospel "to the ends of the earth" (1:8). Still, after focusing so much on Paul, why doesn't Acts tell us what happened to him? (First-century readers probably know more about this question than we do today.)

PART 8

Teaching

Letters Circulate the Message

FOR FIVE WEEKS WE will immerse ourselves in some of the earliest and weightiest of Paul's correspondence with young churches, in the order that they probably were written. In the New Testament these letters are not arranged chronologically but from the longest to the shortest. This arrangement gives priority to Romans, which is surely one of Paul's most significant letters but also may be the last in our possession that he wrote. None of these letters is lightweight, though. Even the shortest is pretty deep.

Summary

    Week 1, Freedom—Paul Encourages Believers

    Week 2, Community—Paul Writes to a Divided Church

    Week 3, Authority—Paul Defends His Mission

    Week 4, Righteous—Paul Says Faith Is Key

    Week 5, Unity—Jew and Gentile Are One in Christ

Paul can be both a joy and a headache to read. Don't beat up on yourself if the meaning of what he says is not immediately obvious. Remember that he is a religious scholar who sometimes writes in the technical language of all scholars. Peter says that Paul writes "according to the wisdom given him," and he admits that some things in Paul's letters are "hard to understand" (2 Pet 3:15–16). That's an understatement!

1

Freedom
Paul Encourages Believers

FIRST THESSALONIANS MAY BE the earliest of Paul's letters. It dates from about 50 CE and is addressed to the church Paul founded at Thessalonica, a strategic port city in Macedonia. Paul's chief purpose is to bolster their faith and their hope of resurrection. He, or perhaps his one of his collaborators, Timothy or Silvanus, elaborates on the same themes in *2 Thessalonians*.

> Rejoice always, pray without ceasing, give thanks in all circumstances; for this is the will of God in Christ Jesus for you.
> —1 Thess 5:16–18

Day 1	1 Thess 1–3	Paul praises the church.
Day 2	1 Thess 4–5	Paul corrects some misconceptions.
Day 3	2 Thess 1–3	Let's go over all that again.

Galatians was written at about the same time as the Thessalonian letters, if not before. It is addressed to churches in Asia Minor. Paul attacks Jewish Christians who contend that gentile converts must become Jews to become true Christians.

> For freedom Christ has set us free. Stand firm, therefore, and do not submit again to a yoke of slavery. —Gal 5:1

PART 8: TEACHING

Day 4	Gal 1:1—2:14	Beware the deceivers.
Day 5	Gal 2:15—3:29	"You foolish Galatians!"
Day 6	Gal 4:1–31	We are adopted into God's family.
Day 7	Gal 5:1—6:18	"Christ has set us free."

Consider...

- The New Testament preserves twenty letters written by first-century missionaries; thirteen of them are attributed to Paul. Because there was no mail service as we know it today, letters were hand-delivered by a trusted messenger. He or she conveyed personal greetings from the sender, read the letter aloud, answered questions, and likely also defended the letter's contents to critics. Knowing this, how would you like to be the one delivering Paul's letter to the Galatians?

- What issue is so important to the Thessalonians that it takes two letters to address?

- Paul appears to expect Christ's return in his lifetime (1 Thess 4:15), though he cannot say when it will occur (5:2). Clearly, it did not happen while he was alive—at least in the way we think he expected it would. Does this failure invalidate his faith? What about ours? Does this caution you about "prophetic" dates and timelines?

- What Paul describes in 1 Thess 4:13–18 is the *parousia* or "coming" of Christ. It is not a "rapture" of believers *out* of this world but the coming of Christ *into* the world. How important is this difference?

- Who is the mysterious "lawless one" of 2 Thess 2:3, 8–9? This figure is apparently not Satan but an agent, or a work, of Satan (2:9). He/she/it might be the antichrist mentioned in 1 John 2:18, 2:22, 4:3, and 2 John 1:7.

- Paul says to "give thanks in all circumstances" (1 Thess 5:18). Note that he says to give thanks *in* all circumstances, not *for* all circumstances. What difference does this make for how you pray?

- Paul says, "Anyone unwilling to work should not eat" (2 Thess 3:10). Taken out of context, this comment might be used against a large variety of people, including those living on pensions and disability. But

FREEDOM

Paul is speaking specifically of those in the Christian community who are "living in idleness" and not contributing to their communal life.

- Paul's letters normally take this form: salutation, thanksgiving, message, closing. What element is missing in his letter to the Galatians? Why is this significant?
- Paul is so angry that he is barely civil to the Galatians (1:6, 3:1). He's not trying to ingratiate himself to them. What is he trying to do?
- Galatians 3:28–29 and 4:4–7 mark a revolutionary statement of Christian freedom, both in Paul's day and in ours. Freedom in Christ is release both from sin and from demands of the law. It is not license to sin anew. Rather, it is submission to the law of Christ—that is, to the law of love, the true intent of the law of Moses. See Gal 5:1 and 5:13–14 and also Rom 8:2 and 1 Cor 9:21. How can we better live into this vision?
- Against the law of Moses, Paul offers the law of love. Against the mark of circumcision, he offers "the marks of Jesus" (Gal 6:17). What are these marks, and how do they reflect the showing of love?
- "The only thing that counts is faith working through love," Paul says (Gal 5:6). The *only* thing?
- The righteous live by faith, Paul says (Gal 3:11). And faith leads to ... (5:6)?
- Paul says he is "in the pain of childbirth" until Christ is formed in the Galatians (4:19). How is Christ formed in us?
- In Gal 5:22–23, Paul lists nine "fruit" (singular) of the Spirit as evidence of a person's new life and the Spirit's indwelling. Can you see such evidence in your life?

2

Community
Paul Writes to a Divided Church

FIRST CORINTHIANS ACTUALLY IS Paul's second letter to the church of Corinth; the first letter has not survived. Paul writes from Ephesus about 53 CE to address specific concerns of the faction-ridden community. Corinth is an important and cosmopolitan Greek city that is notorious for its immorality, partly because it's a port city and also because it's a major center of ritual prostitution connected to worship of the goddess Aphrodite.

> Now I appeal to you, brothers and sisters, by the name of our Lord Jesus Christ, that all of you be in agreement and that there be no divisions among you, but that you be united in the same mind and the same purpose. —1 Cor 1:10

Day 1	1 Cor 1—2:5	Paul appeals for unity.
Day 2	1 Cor 5–6	Paul warns against immorality, disputes.
Day 3	1 Cor 7–8	Paul discusses sexuality.
Day 4	1 Cor 9:1—11:1	Do everything to God's glory.
Day 5	1 Cor 11:2—12:31	Paul writes about orderly worship.
Day 6	1 Cor 13–14	Without love, you've got nothing.
Day 7	1 Cor 15	Our hope is in Christ's resurrection.

Consider...

- Paul always writes to specific people about specific matters. That's especially obvious in 1 Corinthians, where he addresses several stated concerns of members in the divided church. He also conveys truths that are universal and valid everywhere and always. Sometimes it's hard to tell the situation-specific from the universal. Can't we also find some universal in the situation-specific? What happens when we elevate the situation-specific to the status of universal?

- In 1 Cor 7:10, Paul says that a command comes from "not I, but the Lord." In 7:12, he says that a command comes from "I, not the Lord." The first is a teaching that was handed down to him from the Lord; the second is his interpretation. That's not to say it can be ignored. But aren't all his letters mostly his (inspired) interpretation?

- How does 1 Corinthians provide insight into the struggles of early Christians to be faithful to the gospel in a world organized around different values?

- Accused of preaching a diluted gospel, Paul says he gave the Corinthians milk, not solid food, because of their spiritual infancy (3:1–3). Although they have great spiritual gifts (1:7), their divisions show that they still are not mature. On such a maturity scale, how would you rate your church? Are you getting milk or solid food? Can do you grow spiritually on milk alone? Don't you need solid food, too?

- What troubles Paul about the way Corinthians observe the Lord's Supper? How do we observe it differently today? By removing it from a communal meal and making it worship ritual, how have we changed it?

- It is hard to reconcile 14:34–35 ("women should be silent in churches") with 11:5, where women are told to cover their heads while teaching. When Paul addresses what head coverings are "proper" for whom and when (11:3–16), he likely relies on local custom rather than divine inspiration.

- Often read at weddings, the "love chapter" (ch. 13) isn't confined to marriage, is it? How, in fact, does it influence every relationship in one way or another?

- The "male prostitutes" of 6:9 are catamites, boys kept for the sexual pleasure of older men, a fairly common practice of the time in pagan

PART 8: TEACHING

society. Paul's primary concern is prostitution, not same-sex behavior. Does it change your self-perspective to think that "your body is a temple of the Holy Spirit" (6:19)?

- Connect 1:22–25 with Paul's argument for the resurrection in chapter 15.

- Gifts of the Spirit are manifestations of the Holy Spirit that contribute to the common good (12:7). You can find lists of spiritual gifts in 1 Cor 12:4–11 and 28, Rom 12:6–8, and Eph 4:11. Many surveys are available to help you identify your spiritual gifts. Are you aware of your own gifts? Have others confirmed that they see them in you? Are you confirming and nurturing the gifts you have seen in others?

- In the pagan world, most meat sold in public marketplaces was from animals that had been sacrificed to idols. The Jerusalem Council (Acts 15:20–29) sent out a letter telling gentile believers that they should not eat this meat. Paul apparently missed the memo—literally. It seems he learns about it only much later (Acts 21:25). In between times, he tells Corinthians (8:1–13 and 10:23–33) that eating such meat isn't harmful in itself, but they ought to be sensitive to the concerns of those who might be offended by it. The issue is still alive many years later when the book of Revelation quotes Jesus as prohibiting it (Rev 2:14, 20). What do you think of Paul's views on the parameters of Christian freedom?

3

Authority
Paul Defends His Mission

SECOND CORINTHIANS IS PERHAPS Paul's fourth letter to the church at Corinth. It may be a combination of two or more letters. It probably was written about 56 CE, during Paul's final tour of churches. It follows a "painful" visit to the city (2:1) and a hurtful letter to the church (7:8), where many have grown to distrust him. Where 1 Corinthians was concerned about problems in the church, this letter focuses on challenges to Paul's authority and his personal integrity as an apostle. The dramatic shift in tone at chapter 10 may reflect a combining of two letters, or perhaps Paul's growing sense of crisis over his mission and the urgency of defending it vigorously.

> We are afflicted in every way but not crushed; perplexed but not driven to despair; persecuted but not forsaken; struck down but not destroyed; always carrying in the body the death of Jesus so that the life of Jesus may also be made visible in our bodies.
> —2 Cor 4:8-10

Day 1	2 Cor 1–2	Paul reviews his history with the church.
Day 2	2 Cor 3–4	Paul bases his authority on God's grace.
Day 3	2 Cor 5:1—6:13	We walk by faith, not by sight.
Day 4	2 Cor 6:14—7:16	Paul offers comfort in distress.
Day 5	2 Cor 8–9	Paul commends generous givers.
Day 6	2 Cor 10–11	Paul boasts in the Lord.
Day 7	2 Cor 12–13	Power is perfected in weakness.

PART 8: TEACHING

Consider...

- What does the rancor in this letter tell you about Paul's relationship with this church?

- How personally does Paul take events in the church (11:29)?

- Paul's condemnation of his enemies in the church are as bitter as some statements in Galatians. He says his opponents peddle God's word for profit (2:17), proclaim "another Jesus" and "a different gospel" (11:4), and are "false apostles" and agents of Satan (11:13–15). Harsh words! We sometimes hear similar rhetoric in church disputes today. Are you surprised to hear them in the early church, too?

- Paul admits that he lacks formal training as a speaker (11:6) and does not cut a commanding figure (10:1). Are these things important for a preacher? How does Paul suggest he overcomes these weaknesses?

- Paul frankly describes his travails and how close he has come to giving up (1:8–11; 4:8–11, 16–18; and also 6:4–10 and 11:23–28). Are there times when you also feel "unbearably crushed" (1:8) and "afflicted in every way" (5:8)? What sustains you? Have you also learned to "walk by faith and not by sight" (5:7)?

- The "thorn" in Paul's flesh has been the subject of much speculation. Exactly what it was may not matter to us. Can you identify something like it in your own life? If God has not removed it, despite your prayers, do you wonder why not?

- Do you find God's grace sufficient for your shortcomings? Or do you insist on being self-sufficient rather than God-sufficient?

- How is Paul's appeal for a love offering for Jerusalem (chs. 8 and 9) relevant today? Paul urges eager and cheerful giving (8:12, 9:7). But isn't he being manipulative when he sets up a competition among the churches (8:8)?

- He says we should give according to what we have, not according to what we don't have (8:12). How important is this principle to those who are too poor to give much? What does this also suggest about the futility of comparing ourselves to others?

- What do you make of Paul's boasting about his ordeals (chs. 11 and 12)? Does he boast too much? Does he really make a fool of himself (11:16, 12:11)?

AUTHORITY

- For all of its rancor, doesn't this letter contain some great affirmations of faith? Consider (3:17–18, 4:7–9, 5:14–21).
- Explore the ramifications of 5:16–21, especially new creation, reconciliation, and becoming ambassadors for Christ. What is the "human point of view" from which we formerly knew Christ? How does it differ from our new perspective?
- Do you consider yourself an ambassador for Christ? Is your home an embassy of the kingdom? What can you do to better represent Christ?
- What is the veil that Paul suggests covers the eyes of unbelievers when they hear the gospel (3:12—4:6)? How are the faces of Christians unveiled? How can we help others see as well?
- In 13:12 and in several other letters, Paul tells believers to "greet one another with a holy kiss." How would such behavior be viewed in your church today? Is this one of those aspects of first-century culture that is hard to duplicate today?
- Paul concludes his letter with this benediction: "The grace of the Lord Jesus Christ, the love of God, and the communion of the Holy Spirit be with all of you" (13:13). That is a clear affirmation of what will later be called Trinitarian theology. If you think the Bible does not support the concept of Trinity, also check out such passages as Matt 28:19 and Mark 1:9–11.

4

Righteous
Paul Says Faith Is Key

ROMANS IS PAUL'S LONGEST and most influential letter, composed about 57 CE, during his final missionary tour. The letter is intended to introduce Paul and his message to the church in Rome before he visits it. The chief issue he addresses is conflict between Jewish and gentile believers—a problem that exists in other churches and one that Paul views with growing alarm. Romans may be seen as Paul's testament, a valedictory summary of key points in his theology as he prepares for what he is sure will be a showdown in Jerusalem. However, it should be read more as a pastoral response to church problems and less as a systematic statement of theology, something it is not.

> I am not ashamed of the gospel; it is the power of God for salvation in everyone who has faith. —Rom 1:16

Day 1	Rom 1:1—2:16	Paul introduces himself and his message.
Day 2	Rom 2:17—3:31	All have sinned, and all can be saved.
Day 3	Rom 4:1—5:21	We are justified by faith, not by works.
Day 4	Rom 6:1—7:25	We are rescued from sin and the law.
Day 5	Rom 8	We are made heirs with Christ.
Day 6	Rom 9:1—10:4	Jewish unbelief anguishes Paul.
Day 7	Rom 10:5—11:36	God's call is irrevocable.

RIGHTEOUS

Consider...

- Paul's letter to Rome is one of the most influential books in Christian history. Martin Luther, John Wesley, and Karl Barth are among the many who were especially inspired by it. Romans contains many powerful moments but also some dense, almost incomprehensible, passages. Name one or two of each that you find.

- The letter's overall theme, stated masterfully in 1:16–17, is how sinful humans can be brought into right relationship with a holy God. Paul's immediate concern is reconciling Jewish and gentile Christians. He strives to assure gentiles that Jews remain God's covenant people and to assure Jews that God also accepts gentiles.

- To some, 1:26–27 is a blanket condemnation of homosexuality. But the context of these verses is how idolatry twists all human behavior. Paul may be referring specifically to practices in pagan worship. Is anyone *not* included in 1:29–31?

- If you think you made it through the condemnations of chapter 1 unscathed, 2:1 is a "Gotcha!" Whoever you are, you have no more excuse than anyone else.

- Chapter 1 appears to be directed to gentiles in Rome's churches, and chapter 2 to Jews. The "Gotcha!" of 2:1, leads into the general "all have sinned" of 3:21–25. Can you see how the whole letter is aimed at reconciling Jew and gentile believers?

- "There is no one who is righteous, not even one," Paul says in 3:10, drawing from similar statements in Hebrew Scriptures. Yet in 1:17 and in Gal 3:11 and elsewhere, he insists that "the one who is righteous will live by faith," quoting Hab 2:4. Who or what can make you righteous?

- Do you understand what a great privilege it is that you are a child of God who can cry "Abba!" to your Heavenly Father (8:15–17)?

- What has the power to separate us from the love of Christ (8:31–35)? Does this mean that you can behave however you wish with no fear of breaking the relationship? Or simply that God will not give up on you however stubborn you are?

- Paul is distressed that so few of his fellow Jews trust in Jesus, but he maintains hope for them because "the gifts and the calling of God are irrevocable" (11:29).
- How does the image of grafted branches illustrate Paul's argument (11:17–24)?
- If God's call to Jews is still valid (11:29), are attempts to convert them to Christianity valid? Do they "need" converting? Can Christians still share their faith with Jews?
- When Paul says we are justified by faith, "apart from works prescribed by the law" (3:28), what kind of works does he mean?
- Paul says God's nature is revealed throughout creation (1:18–21) and God's law is written on human hearts through conscience (1:32, 2:14–15) so that even those who don't know the law formally still may follow its spirit (2:14). Do these statements ring true for you? Do you know nonbelievers who behave better than some believers? What does creation tell you about God's nature? Do you experience "nature" as positive and supportive or negative and threatening?
- What does being "predestined" (8:29–30) mean to you? Does it mean that you were chosen by God for salvation while others were chosen for condemnation? Don't *you* have anything to do with this? If it was all decided ahead of time, how can any choice you made be your fault—and how can any be to your credit? If it's all decided ahead of time, and can't be changed, what does it matter how you live? Or is being "predestined" mean that you realize that you were chosen for salvation, just as all others were, and you celebrate knowing that you are saved?

5

Unity
Jew and Gentile Are One in Christ

> For there is no distinction between Jew and Greek; the same Lord is Lord of all and is generous to all who call on him. —Rom 10:12

Day 1	Rom 12:1—14:12	Be transformed, not conformed.
Day 2	Rom 14:13—15:13	Please others, not yourself.
→ *Deeper*	Rom 16	See how many people Paul knows in Rome!

Ephesians is a circular letter to churches that Paul has heard about but never visited. The address "to the Ephesians" appears to be a late, and incorrect, identification because Paul ministered in Ephesus for years. One ancient tradition identifies it as the letter to churches in Laodicea mentioned in Col 4:16. Some scholars think this letter is not Paul's but the work of a disciple writing as Paul's representative.

> For by grace you have been saved through faith, and this is not your own doing; it is the gift of God—not the result of works, so that no one may boast. —Eph 2:8-9

Day 3	Eph 1:1—2:10	We are God's adopted children.
Day 4	Eph 2:11—3:21	Once aliens, we are strangers no more.
Day 5	Eph 4	One body, one Spirit, one Lord.

PART 8: TEACHING

Day 6	Eph 5	Be imitators of God.
Day 7	Eph 6	Put on God's armor against evil.

Consider...

- What are the limits of Paul's favorable attitude toward government (Rom 13:1–7)? Is Paul saying that *anything* a government body does is pleasing to God? (Compare this with 1 Pet 2:13–15. Also consider the overall negative attitude of the book of Revelation.) Don't we love government when it seems to be in our favor and hate it otherwise?

- What does Paul change when he repeats the "love command" of Jesus (Rom 13:9–10)? What significance do you see in this change?

- In Romans, Paul speaks of the law many times, not always in ways that are easy to follow. Though he says Christians are free from the law's demands, he insists that the Hebrew Scriptures are still useful for Christians (15:4). How do you find these Scriptures encouraging and full of hope?

- Romans 12–15 is full of practical advice. Any of it stand out to you?

- Who are the strong and the weak in Rom 14 and 15? And the weak in 5:6? Why or why not are they the same?

- Paul clearly believes that the dawning of God's salvation is closer than ever before (13:11–12). Can it happen without some cataclysmic event?

- Romans 16 lists some of the believers in Rome whom Paul already knows. Is it surprising that he knows so many already, or that several of them are women? (*Note:* In 16:7, Junia is, and always has been, female. The male *Junias* in some versions is a patriarchal fiction intended to hide Junia's identity.)

- What is the "mystery" of Christ (Eph 3:3–6 and Col 1:26)? Isn't this also the "secret" of 1 Cor 2:7–8 and Rom 16:25–26, as well as Mark 4:11?

- Christians need to be strong in the Lord because they do not struggle merely against human enemies but also against what the KJV calls "powers and principalities" (Eph 6:12). These cosmic forces of evil are active throughout the universe and entrenched in human social structures. Could these include your church?

- What's the "armor" we can put on to protect ourselves (Eph 6:13–17)? Aren't these spiritual practices rather than physical body armor and weaponry?
- "Wives, be subject to your husbands" (Eph 5:22) sounds very one-sided. But doesn't Paul affirm the mutuality of husband and wife in 5:21, 25, and 33?
- If head and body are part of the same organism, what does it mean to say that Christ is the "head" of the church, which is his body (Eph 5:21–30)?
- The role of apostles, prophets, evangelists, pastors, and teachers is not to *do* the work of ministry of the church but to "*equip the saints* for the work of ministry" (4:11–12). Are there those in your church who think church staff should do it all? Indeed, aren't some church models based on that premise?
- In the original Greek, the doxological passage 1:3–14 is one long and very complicated sentence. Isn't it also a pretty good summary of Paul's gospel?
- Note the movement from Father to Son to Holy Spirit in 1:3–14 and the reverse in 4:4–6. Without using a word not invented yet, Trinity again!
- Ephesians is rich in memorable phrases—"For by grace you have been saved through faith" (2:8–9); "You are no longer strangers and aliens" (2:19); "I, therefore, the prisoner in the Lord, beg you to lead a life worthy of the calling to which you have been called" (4:1); "There is one body and one Spirit" (4:4); "Be angry but do not sin" (4:26); "Be imitators of God" (5:1). Do you find others?

PART 9

Coaching
More Dispatches Carry the Word

IN THE NEXT FIVE weeks, we will read more dispatches from the front lines of Christian mission in the early days of the church. Each letter or sermon offers advice and encouragement to believers. Some of these letters are by the apostle Paul, some by others, and at least one comes to us from an unknown hand.

Summary

Week 1, Renewal—Dimensions of Christian Living

Week 2, Guidance—Advice for Two Pastors

Week 3, Mediator—Jesus Is Our Forerunner

Week 4, Faith—Love in Action

Week 5, Unwavering—Assurance for Embattled Believers

You may be familiar with several of the books we're about to read but probably not with all of them. When was the last time you heard a sermon preached from Titus? Or Jude? Hebrews is fun to quote from, but it's hard to tell what's going on between the quotes. However well-acquainted you are with them, each of these fourteen books has something important to tell you about staying faithful to Christ in your life. Enjoy the diversity of expression but uniformity of message that you encounter here!

1

Renewal
Dimensions of Christian Living

PAUL WRITES TO THE *Philippians* from one prison or another, possibly in Rome. The church at Philippi in Macedonia holds a special place in his heart. He calls it "my joy and my crown" (4:1). This is one of his warmest letters.

> I thank my God every time I remember you, constantly praying with joy in every one of my prayers for all of you, because of your sharing in the gospel from the first day until now. —Phil 1:3–5

Day 1	Phil 1	Paul proclaims Christ boldly.
Day 2	Phil 2:1–18	Take on the mind of Christ.
	Phil 3:1–11	I want to know Christ.
Day 3	Phil 3:12—4:20	Press on toward the goal.

Colossians probably dates from the same time as Philippians, though some scholars think it was written by a later disciple of Paul. Colossae was a prosperous but declining trade center in Asia Minor. The letter opposes false teachers—probably gnostics, who taught that salvation was possible only through secret *gnosis*, or knowledge.

> So if you have been raised with Christ, seek the things that are above, where Christ is, seated at the right hand of God. —Col 3:1

PART 9: COACHING

Day 4	Col 1	We are reconciled to God through Christ.
Day 5	Col 2	Don't be deceived by false teachers.
Day 6	Col 3:1—4:6	Put on a new life in Christ.
Day 7	Phlm	Paul goes to bat for a friend who's in trouble.

Consider...

- Philippians has been called Paul's "letter of joy" because he mentions joy and rejoicing fourteen times in twenty-nine verses (a few less times in some translations). He's writing from a prison cell. What's he got to be so joyful about?

- Philippi is a Roman colony in which there apparently are few Jews, so Paul never quotes from the Hebrew Scriptures in this letter. Did you notice this lack while reading it? Does this show you how Christianity can flourish without an obvious Jewish anchor? Even if the anchor isn't obvious, can you see how it's still there?

- In Phil 3:7, Paul says that whatever gains he had before Christ, "these I have come to regard as loss because of Christ." The word translated "loss" here is sometimes rendered as "trash." It's actually a much earthier expression. Can you see why Bibles meant for public reading are careful here? But what's wrong with earthiness?

- Paul wants believers to be "of the same mind," and that is the mind of Christ (Phil 2:1–5). What are some implications of having such a mind? Does it mean that we all agree on everything?

- What does it mean to say that "our citizenship is in heaven" (Phil 3:20)? Do we have a sort of dual citizenship with this world? If so, which has priority?

- Paul may be quoting familiar hymns in Phil 2:6–11, which tells of Christ's humiliation and exaltation, and Col 1:15–20, which tells of Christ's supremacy. Can you imagine trying to sing them?

- Colossians has many similarities to Ephesians, though some doubt Paul wrote either. Can you see how the letters resemble each other?

- In Col 3:18–19, Paul appears to contradict his teaching on marriage mutuality in Eph 5:21 and 1 Cor 7:4. Or is he just wording it differently?

- Colossians has many memorable moments, such as, "He has rescued us from the power of darkness" (1:13); "He is the image of the invisible God" (1:15); "In him the whole fullness of deity dwells bodily" (2:9); "You have stripped off the old self" (3:9–10); "As God's chosen ones, holy and beloved, cloth yourselves with compassion" (3:12).

- Philemon is often called a masterpiece of discretion. Paul never quite states what he expects, but he still makes his intentions clear. Walk through Paul's careful appeal for the full acceptance of the slave Onesimus. Why is he so cautious?

- Paul makes a personal appeal, but he also applies social pressure because his letter comes from Timothy as well as Paul, and it's addressed not only to Philemon but also to the church that meets in Philemon's home. If Philemon had rejected Paul's request, would the letter have been preserved?

- Slavery contradicts his gospel (Gal 3:28), but Paul seems to accept it as a social institution (see Col 3:22). Do you think he could, or should, have opposed it outright?

- Paul appeals to Philemon on the basis of a higher law—the law of Christ. He suggests that new relationships in Christ can transform existing social relationships. Have you seen evidence of such transformation in your own life or community?

- Paul frequently refers to himself and others as "slaves" or "servants" of Christ? What is this language trying to affirm about a person's relationship with Christ? In light of continuing contention over slavery, can you see how this language confuses some people?

2

Guidance
Advice for Two Pastors

THE BOOKS OF *1 and 2 Timothy* and *Titus* are called "Pastoral Epistles" because they are letters of pastoral advice for two disciples of Paul. Titus and 1 Timothy are hard to fit into the chronology of Paul's life but may date to about 55 CE. Second Timothy could come from Paul's imprisonment in Rome. Some date it later, though, theorizing that Paul was released after trial in Rome and carried out another missionary journey that included Spain before he was arrested again. Other scholars think all three are the work of a later disciple of Paul, writing under his name, rather than Paul himself.

> Remember Jesus Christ raised from the dead, a descendant of David—that is my gospel. —2 Tim 2:8

Day 1	1 Tim 1	Timothy is told to "fight the good fight."
Day 2	1 Tim 2:1—3:13	Instructions on worship and leadership.
Day 3	1 Tim 3:14—5:2	More on spiritual training and doctrine.
→ *Deeper*	1 Tim 5:3–24	Instructions for widows, elders, and slaves.
Day 4	1 Tim 6:1–21	Guard the treasure entrusted to you.
Day 5	2 Tim 1–2	Accept suffering without shame.
Day 6	2 Tim 3–4	"I have finished the race."
Day 7	Titus 1–3	Be a model for others.

Consider...

- The Timothy letters bug some scholars because some parts sound very much like the Paul we know from other letters, and some parts don't. Does 2 Tim 4:6–8 passage sound convincingly Pauline to you?
- First Timothy waffles about the role of women in the church. On the one hand (2:11–12), Paul wants wives (or maybe all women) to "learn in silence" from their husbands (or maybe any man). On the other hand, 3:11 may imply that there are women deacons in the Ephesian church, just as there are in the Roman church (Rom 16:1).
- Review the "This saying is sure" (or "trustworthy") sayings (1 Tim 1:15, 3:1, 4:9, 2 Tim 2:11, Titus 3:8). Are there others that you could add to convey the essence of true faith?
- In 1 Tim 2:3–4, Paul asserts that God "desires everyone to be saved and to come to the knowledge of the truth." Do you think God will get what God desires? If so, how?
- Think through the bizarre argument in 1 Tim 2:13–15. If Eve was deceived by Satan, she is guilty only of being deceived. If Adam was not deceived, however, he is guilty of willfully rebelling against God. How does that make him superior to Eve and qualified to teach anyone anything? What does childbearing have to do with it?
- The text of 2 Tim 3:16 is often cited as a proof text for biblical authority. But only the Hebrew Scriptures existed then, so the New Testament isn't included, except by a questionable extension. The text also says nothing about how inspiration occurs and what its full implications are. Besides, isn't all life "God-breathed"? (See Ps 33:6, Ps 104:29–30, Gen 1:30, Gen 2:7, Acts 17:25.)
- In 1 Tim 5:23, Paul tells Timothy to drink "a little wine" as well as water after suffering from the first-century equivalent of Montezuma's revenge. So much for total abstinence.
- Persecution comes with the territory, Paul says (2 Tim 3:12). If you are faithful, you'll get hurt, while many evildoers will skate through life unscathed. (Echoes of Ecclesiastes!) Does this sound true in your experience?
- Both 1 Timothy (3:1–13) and Titus (1:5) talk about choosing church officers but never say what they actually do. The result is varied

- practice and general confusion among denominations throughout history. Despite what some claim, Scripture never says much about how churches should be run, or by whom.

- Both 1 and 2 Timothy quote from familiar hymns or liturgies: "For there is one God and one mediator" (1 Tim 2:5–6); "He was revealed in the flesh" (1 Tim 3:16); and "If we have died with him . . ." (2 Tim 2:11–13).

- Second Timothy sounds like a last testament or valedictory statement, written with death clearly in view. See especially 4:6–8. Do you have Paul's confidence at this point in your life?

- It is not known when Paul visited Crete (Titus 1:5) or wintered in Nicopolis (3:12). These visits may have occurred during a gap in the Acts chronology or during Paul's hypothetical fourth missionary journey after release from jail in Rome.

- Titus 1:12–13 repeats an ethnic slur attributed to Epimenides of Crete. It creates a famous paradox: if all Cretans are liars, can you believe a Cretan who says so? Still, you may wonder how such a slander got into the Bible at all. You don't have to be Cretan to sense something awry here.

3

Mediator

Jesus Is Our Forerunner

FOLLOWING THE PAULINE LETTERS in the New Testament are the "Catholic" or "General" Epistles, so called because they are addressed to no particular community. The book of *Hebrews* is the work of an anonymous second-generation Christian (2:3). Although some early commentators attribute the work to Paul, others favor Barnabas or Apollos. The early church authority Origen said "only God knows" the author's identity.[1] It is less a letter than a sermon, intended to strengthen Jewish converts who are distressed by threats of persecution. It may date from the mid to late 60s CE, or perhaps much later.

> For we do not have a high priest who is unable to sympathize with our weaknesses, but we have one who in every respect has been tested, as we are, yet without sin. —Heb 4:15

Day 1	Heb 1–2	Jesus is the pioneer of our salvation.
Day 2	Heb 3–5	Jesus is our great high priest.
Day 3	Heb 6–7	One sacrifice covers all our sins.
Day 4	Heb 8–9	Jesus makes a new covenant with us.
Day 5	Heb 10	You need assurance and confidence.
Day 6	Heb 11	Faith is central to everything.
Day 7	Heb 12–13	Don't grow weary or lose heart.

---

1. Eusebius, *Church History* 6.25.14.

PART 9: COACHING

Consider...

- Hebrews offers encouragement to Jewish Christians facing persecution. Its argument is dense, highly philosophical, and often very hard to follow. Even the author admits that his argument may be lost on some readers (5:11-14). He blames such lack of understanding on spiritual immaturity. Your reaction to this claim?

- The same God who spoke to our ancestors "long ago" (1:1) speaks to us "in these last days" (1:2)—that is, in the age inaugurated by the Messiah—about what is to happen in "the coming world" (2:5), when Messiah reigns. The God of the Bible does not change identities between the testaments. Continuity is assured by the Son, "the exact imprint of God's very being," through whom all things are created (1:2-3).

- Although parts of Hebrews can be tough sledding for most readers, parts of it are quite beautiful. What are your favorite passages?

- The author commends faith—"the assurance of things hoped for, the conviction of things not seen" (11:1). Abram left his homeland not knowing where God was leading him (11:8). Similarly, those who persevere in faith will inherit "a kingdom that cannot be shaken" (12:28). Do these words help boost your confidence?

- In Heb 4:12-13, the term *logos* (or "word") does not refer to Scripture (as is so often claimed) but to the Living Word that God speaks throughout Scripture and most definitively through Jesus. The "it" that many translations insert twice in verse 12 is misleading and not at all necessary, as the King James and some very literal translations show. And the next reference, in verse 13, is to "him," not to an "it"— the "him" being "the one to whom we must render an account"—God and Christ, certainly not any book, even a book of Scripture.

- Hebrews argues against any human priesthood. So why has the church almost always had priests or an equivalent office? (It can be argued that all churches have the functional equivalent of priests.)

- Though Christ is "holy and blameless" (7:26) and "without sin" (4:15), he was "made perfect" through suffering (2:10, 5:9). Can you understand this in terms of his perfect identification with humanity? Otherwise, how can one blameless be made perfect?

- As our holy and blameless high priest, Christ makes one perfect sacrifice that is sufficient for all time, rendering all other sacrifices superfluous (7:26–28; 9:11–14, 25–26). Thus he makes a new covenant with humanity that is better than the first covenant made at Sinai (8:6–7) This is the new covenant proclaimed by the prophet Jeremiah, when God promised to "put my laws in their minds and write them on their hearts" (Jer 31:31–33). This new covenant renders the first one obsolete, and it "will soon disappear" (Heb 8:13). This is not, as is often claimed, "supersessionism" (the idea that Christianity replaces Judaism) because Hebrews nowhere claims that God has revoked the promises of the first covenant (Rom 11:29).

- Melchizedek (first mentioned in 5:6) is a mysterious priest-king who appears briefly in Gen 14:17–20. Alluding to Ps 110:4, Hebrews says he points to Jesus. Such obscure references either impress Bible readers or leave them cold. What's your reaction? Who is this guy, and why do we care?

- We tend to understand the word *discipline* as a form of punishment. But read Heb 12:5–11, substituting the words *correct*, *educate*, or *train*. Also see Prov 3:11–12. Do you resent such discipline?

4

Faith

Love in Action

THE LETTER OF *JAMES* presumably is the work of the brother of Jesus who led the church at Jerusalem. It appears to be addressed to Jewish Christians. Because the issue of gentile converts is never mentioned, it may have been written before the Jerusalem Council in 48 or 49 CE. If it was, it is the earliest book of the New Testament. It is a homily of general ethical instruction built around the theme of faith in action.

> Be doers of the word, and not merely hearers who deceive themselves. —Jas 1:22

Day 1	Jas 1:1—2:13	Be doers of the word, not just hearers.
Day 2	Jas 2:14—3:18	Faith without works is dead.
Day 3	Jas 4–5	Purify your hearts.

The three letters of John appear to form a package. *Third John* is the cover letter, written to an individual. *Second John* is intended to be read to a congregation to introduce *1 John*, which is a sermon of advice for a community split by disputes over the nature of Jesus. The author, who identifies himself only as "the Elder," probably also wrote the Fourth Gospel. The letters cannot be dated precisely but could come as early as the 60s CE.

Day 4	3 John	"The Elder" writes two brief letters...
	2 John	...warning church leaders about deceivers.
Day 5	1 John 1:1—2:17	In God there is no darkness at all.
Day 6	1 John 2:18—3:24	Let us love in truth and action.
Day 7	1 John 4–5	Abide in love, not fear.

Consider...

- Martin Luther dismissed James as "an epistle of straw" compared with the other epistles,[1] and because he read Jas 2:14–26 as an attack on Paul's doctrine of justification by faith. It is often stated that Paul says we are saved by faith alone but James says faith requires works. Are Paul and James really so far apart in what they say? (For Paul's view, compare Rom 1:17 with Gal 5:6.)

- The "scattered" or "dispersed" tribes of 1:1 may be diaspora Jews in general, but more likely they are Christians who make up the new Israel. See also 1 Pet 1:1.

- What does James mean by being double-minded (1:8, 4:8)? For an excellent example, see Rom 7:15–25.

- "Be doers of the word and not merely hearers," James says (1:22). In one ear and out the other isn't enough. If you don't *do*, can you really say you have *heard*?

- James says that conflicts among people, and sin in general, arise from "cravings that are at war within you" (Jas 4:1). You want something, and you kill to get it. Is this why the tenth commandment tells us not to want what doesn't belong to us?

- What is "the royal law" (Jas 2:8) and "the perfect law, the law of liberty" (1:25)?

- Life is a mist that quickly vanishes, says Jas 4:13–15. Heard this before?

---

1. Luther, *Preface to the New Testament 1545 (1522)*, in *Works of Martin Luther*, 6:444.

- "How plain, how full, and how deep a compendium of genuine Christianity," John Wesley said of 1 John.[2] Can you see why it is one of the New Testament's most popular books?

- When we walk in the light of Christ, we have fellowship with him and with one another (1 John 1:7). The word translated "fellowship" is *koinonia*, also meaning "partnership" or "sharing." It's something a community can find only through Christ. Potlucks and the like help build fellowship, but there's more to it, isn't there?

- Consider line by line the magnificent passage 1 John 4:7–21. We show our love for God, whom we cannot see, by our love for our brothers and sisters, whom we *can* see. Can you state Jesus' central message of love any better than this?

- Only John's letters mention "antichrists" (1 John 2:18, 22; 4:3; 2 John 7). Who are they? What do they deny? Are they still around today?

- Starting at 2:3, John uses the word "know" more than forty times to combat the claims of church dissidents that they have special *gnosis*, or knowledge. These believers, influenced by Greek philosophy, saw a strict division between flesh and spirit. Among other things, they said that Christ could not have taken on human flesh but only *appeared* to be human and could not suffer and die (1 John 4:1–3, 2 John 7). This heresy became known as *docetism* (from the Greek word meaning "to appear"). Several New Testament letters (Col, 1 and 2 Tim, Titus) hint that this is the heresy they are combatting. Is it still active today? Name several major doctrines it undermines.

- Against the new teaching of the dissidents, the Elder proclaims "what you heard from the beginning" (2:24) about the physical nature of Christ (1:1–3). He repeats the old/new command also "heard from the beginning"—that they love one another (2:7, 3:11).

- "Test the spirits," says 1 John 4:1, to see whether they are from God or from false prophets. How can you best do this? Is this different from the kind of "judging" that Jesus tells us not to do (Matt 7:1 and elsewhere)?

---

2. John Wesley, *Journal*, Sept. 1, 1763, in *The Works of the Reverend John Wesley* (New York: Waugh and Mason, 1835), 4:158.

5

Unwavering
Assurance for Embattled Believers

First Peter is written from "Babylon" (Rome) to believers in Asia Minor, comforting converts who feel like aliens in their own culture. Because of the letter's sophisticated Greek, it's been suggested that Silvanus (Silas) may be the actual author, writing in Peter's name (5:12). *Second Peter* appears to be a testament or summary of Peter's teaching, perhaps written by another disciple of Peter. *Jude* identifies himself as the brother of James, presumably the James who led the church at Jerusalem and wrote the letter of James. If that is so, Jude must also be a brother of Jesus. These letters could date from the early 60s CE, although many scholars think 2 Peter is a much later work.

> Like living stones, let yourselves be built into a spiritual house, to be a holy priesthood, to offer spiritual sacrifices acceptable to God through Jesus Christ. —1 Pet 2:5

Day 1	1 Pet 1:1—2:10	God makes us a royal priesthood.
Day 2	1 Pet 2:11—3:22	Always be ready to tell others about God's love.
Day 3	1 Pet 4–5	Give your cares to God.
Day 4	Jude 1:1–24	Contend for the faith, Jude says.
Day 5	2 Pet 1	Here is a call to godly living.
Day 6	2 Pet 2	Here is a warning against false teachers.
Day 7	2 Pet 3	Here is a warning against scoffers.

PART 9: COACHING

Consider...

- Whoever wrote 1 Peter, the letter offers great comfort and encouragement and many memorable images. What are some of your favorite passages?

- First Peter is written to those who are "aliens and exiles" in their own world (1:1, 2:11). What makes them feel this way?

- Christ gives us "a new birth into a living hope" (1 Pet 1:3). What is this hope?

- What does Peter mean by calling women "the weaker sex" (1 Pet 3:7)? His intent is to honor women as coheirs of God's salvation. Nevertheless, the notion may feel grating today. In Peter's day, women were considered inherently weaker both physically and intellectually, and their weakness was socially enforced. Today women are still disadvantaged by social convention, but don't we see more clearly now that this is an imposed weakness, not an inherent one?

- The text of 1 Pet 3:19-20 and 4:6 are among the likely sources of the statement in some versions of the Apostles' Creed that Jesus "descended into hell." Is that what Peter is saying?

- First Peter says believers should "accept the authority of every human institution" so they can't be accused of being lawbreakers (2:13-15). This is similar to Paul's statement in Rom 13:1-7. But note the contrast with Peter's attitude in Acts 4:19-20. What's the gist of all this?

- Why is personal testimony (2 Pet 1:16-21) so important?

- In 1 Pet 2:11—3:12 a conventional household code of conduct is offered that is similar to that of the Pastoral Epistles. Though this code accepts the rigid social hierarchy of the time, it may suggest changes ahead. Note the repetition of "in the same way" in 3:1, 7.

- Are you "always ready to make your defense to anyone who demands from you an accounting for the hope that is in you" (1 Pet 3:15)?

- No prophecy of Scripture is a matter of private interpretation or human will, 2 Pet 1:20-21 says, but all prophecy comes from inspiration by the Holy Spirit. Remember, prophecy is not prediction but proclamation of the message of God, "the word of the Lord." But how can you know what is real and what is false, what is "a lamp shining in a dark place" (2 Pet 1:19) and what comes from false prophets? This requires discernment!

- How is God "not slow about his promise" (2 Pet 3:9)? Don't we, like those in Peter's day, get tired of waiting for promises to be fulfilled?
- "The day of the Lord will come like a thief," 2 Pet 3:10 says, echoing a common chord in the New Testament. Then it speaks of cosmic cataclysms that include either the *destruction* or the *purification* of earth. Which do you think is more likely?
- The text of 2 Pet 2:20–22 suggests that it is better that you never knew Christ at all than to have known him and turned back to your former way of life. What implications does this have for evangelism and discipleship?
- There is some relationship between 2 Peter and Jude, though we can't be sure what it is. One could have borrowed from the other, or they both borrowed from the same source. Note the similarities between 2 Pet 2:1–18 and 3:2–3 and Jude 4–18.
- What false teachers or teaching does Jude warn the church about?
- Jude 14–16 quotes from the book of Enoch. It was known to several early Christian authors, but it is recognized as Scripture today only by the Ethiopian Orthodox Church. Does it have to be Scripture to be truthful?
- Take a few moments to admire Jude's concluding doxology (vv. 24–25).

PART 10

Unveiling

Visions Show God at Work in History

THE BOOK OF REVELATION winds up the Bible's story by showing us what's going on behind the scenes of human history. What a wild ride this is! We'll spend two weeks unraveling a few of the mysteries of this endlessly fascinating and frustrating book.

Summary

Week 1, Endurance—Stay Faithful to the End

Week 2, Triumph—God Wins!

Revelation is one of the most abused books of the Bible. It is not, and was never intended to be, a blueprint for the future. It's mostly about surviving the present. It's written to encourage seven churches facing adversity, and these churches stand for all churches, then and now. Revelation 1:1 says God "signified" (KJV) the message to John of Patmos—that is, conveyed it in symbols. That means everything in Revelation is symbolic. To take it "literally" is to miss the point entirely. Everything John describes is only "like" his description, John says more than forty times. That is, everything in it is a symbolic pointer to the truth. So "decoding" Revelation requires imaginative reconstruction of a new symbolic world with Christ at the center. If the Bible is the story of God bringing humans to salvation, Revelation is a colorful pageant celebrating the story's triumphant conclusion.

1

Endurance
Stay Faithful to the End

REVELATION IS WRITTEN TO seven churches in what today is Turkey to warn them against corruption by idolatrous Roman culture and to strengthen them against fear of persecution. The book is dated by ancient authorities about 95 CE and is sometimes attributed to John the apostle. Like the book of Daniel, it uses ancient and often bizarre imagery to portray oppression as part of the age-old struggle of good against evil. Its purpose is not to predict events of a distant future but to assure believers that God is in control of history, evil empires cannot stand forever, and faithfulness will be rewarded. It is thus a fitting ending to the cosmic drama that started with Genesis.

Here is a call for the endurance and faith of the saints. —Rev 13:10

Day 1	Rev 1	John receives a "revelation of Jesus Christ."
Day 2	Rev 2	Christ has messages for the seven churches.
Day 3	Rev 3	Each church hears words of judgment (evaluation).
Day 4	Rev 4–5	John sees God's throne.
Day 5	Rev 6–7	Seven seals are broken.
Day 6	Rev 8–9	Seven trumpets sound the call.
Day 7	Rev 10–11	Seven thunders are muffled.

PART 10: UNVEILING

Consider...

- Some commentators date Revelation to the reign of the Emperor Domitian (81–96 CE), others to the turmoil following the death of Nero (68–69 CE). Good arguments can be made for either date. In both periods, Christians were not persecuted widely but were under great pressure to follow pagan rather than Christian lifestyles.

- Note that it's the book of Revelation, *singular*, not "Revelations," plural. It is one singular and continuous revelation. What implications does that have for interpreting it?

- Though it is supposed to be an "unveiling" of truth, Revelation may be the most veiled book of the Bible. Its complex "apocalyptic" style is dazzling but often hard to understand. What do you think is going on here?

- Do you see parallels between the situations of the seven churches and the situations in some churches today? Are these common problems throughout history? Is that one reason Revelation has always been so relevant?

- How is chapter 4 the heart of this revelation of Jesus Christ? What does it reveal about Christ and the nature of reality?

- "Here is a call for the endurance of the saints," John says (14:12), so his theme is "Persevere! Endure!" John tries to bolster the faith of his readers by centering them on Christ, who is the central figure of the book. It's a revelation from God, about Christ, to those too weak to stand against empire and in danger of losing hope.

- Revelation is a kaleidoscope of sometimes grotesque images illustrating how God works in our world. John's frequent use of the terms *as* and *like* indicate that he cannot literally describe or explain what he sees in his visions, and we should be cautious about trying to pin down a literal meaning to the images. It is too easy to read current events into his symbols—as people have been doing for nineteen hundred years. Revelation lifts the veil that conceals the meaning of events. It does not reveal a timeline for the future. Why do we seek such timelines and "blueprints"?

- John's visions concern "what is, and what is to take place after this" (1:19). Does that mean his visions are going to "predict" the future, or will they reveal truths about how the world works and will continue to work until Christ returns in final victory?

- The "four horsemen of the apocalypse" don't predict the future. They have galloped throughout human history. What evidence of them do you see in our time, as well as in the ages before us?
- What do the seals tell us about how God acts to redeem humans from captivity to sin? How do the trumpets parallel the seals?
- Everything in Revelation happens in sevens because seven is the number of completeness. Name some sevens you've noticed so far. More are coming.
- Hymns and doxologies frequently interrupt the narrative. Of special note are those in 4:8–11; 5:9–14; 7:10, 12; 11:15–18; 12:10–12; 15:3–4; and 19:6–8. How many of these do you recognize in hymns and songs of the church?
- In his messages to Pergamum and Thyatira (2:14 and 2:20–21), Christ denounces the eating of food sacrificed to idols. This may be an attack on Paul, who gives somewhat different advice in 1 Cor 8:1–13 and 10:25–33
- Where does the "rapture" fit into the story Revelation tells? Does it fit in at all? If Revelation is a "blueprint" of the future, why isn't the rapture in there?

2

Triumph
God Wins!

John's visions do not tell a consecutive story. They repeat the same story from different perspectives so that a complete picture of events emerges only at the end. Chapters 6 and 7 tell the basic story, which concludes in chapters 21 and 22.

> And the one who was seated on the throne said, "See, I am making all things new." —Rev 21:5

Day 1	Rev 12–13	Here's a peek behind the cosmic battle.
Day 2	Rev 14–15	It's judgment time.
Day 3	Rev 16–17	Seven bowls of wrath are poured out.
Day 4	Rev 18	Babylon is destroyed.
Day 5	Rev 19	Christ rides to victory.
Day 6	Rev 20	One thousand years and judgment.
Day 7	Rev 21–22	Creation is renewed.

Consider...

- Chapters 12 and 13 raise the veil to allow us to see the cosmic battle behind the scenes. Who is the "woman clothed with the sun" (Rev 12:1)? Who is her child? Why must they be protected from the dragon?
- There are many symbols in Revelation—some of them quite obscure—but there is broad agreement among Bible scholars about what

most of the symbols mean. When you study Revelation, avoid sectarian resources that lead you down the rabbit hole into cramped little worlds that are far stranger and far more dangerous than anything the real Revelation reveals.

- How do the seven bowls of wrath parallel and intensify the seven seals and seven trumpets? What does this repetition mean?
- The second beast is a seductive and deceptive political figure. What powers does it display? Do you see them at work today?
- What is the "mark of the beast" and what does it have to do with the name of the beast (13:17, 14:11)? By contrast, what is the seal of God (7:2, 3; 9:4)? Is the mark a cruel parody of the seal?
- If seven is a perfect number, 666 is a three-way loser. But it's still a powerful figure. Originally (for reasons your study Bible may tell you), the numbers probably stood for the evil Emperor Nero. Are there similar figures at work today?
- The beast certainly works against Christ, but the term "antichrist" appears nowhere in Revelation. Does it matter that Revelation, the final "revelation" of the Bible, doesn't clarify all the Bible's terminology and answer all our questions?
- The forces of evil assemble in 16:16 for a final battle at Harmagedon, "the mount of Megiddo." Megiddo sits in a strategic place in a broad plain. Many key battles were fought here before the site was abandoned. But there is no mount here, only a *tell*, a pile of dead cities built atop one another. What is John hinting at with this reference?
- *Babylon* is a code name for any place opposed to God's rule. Rome is Babylon. Are there others? Can you name a Babylon of today?
- Babylon and new Jerusalem exist at the same time. Believers are told to "come out" of Babylon (18:4). How do you "come out" and move from one to the other? Can you live in both at the same time?
- In chapter 13, two beasts appear to do the dragon's bidding, forming a sort of evil trinity. In what other ways does Revelation suggest that evil is a parody of good?
- Think of new Jerusalem in the same way you think of the kingdom of God. It's here, but it's not yet here fully. It has yet to bear its full promise.

PART 10: UNVEILING

- Why must John be rebuked *twice* for trying to worship an angel (19:10 and 22:8–9)?

- It's easy to get lost in the weeds in Revelation. Remember, this is not a road map. The twists and turns don't necessarily add up the way you think they might, if they "add up" at all. Name some loose ends you'd like to have neatly tied up in a pretty bow.

- Revelation is frank in its depiction of evil that will not go away. But it insists that God is with us all the way, and that God will triumph in the end. Do you find this message comforting, even if it's not very cheerful?

- If the Bible is the story of God bringing creation to its intended goal, do you see Revelation as a fitting conclusion?

www.ingramcontent.com/pod-product-compliance
Lightning Source LLC
Chambersburg PA
CBHW072127160426
43197CB00012B/2024